FOREST WALK ON A FRIDAY

STORIES ON LOVE, HOME AND FINDING MY VOICE AT MIDLIFE

LYNNE GOLODNER

SCOTIA ROAD BOOKS

Forest Walk on a Friday by Lynne Golodner

First published in 2025 by Scotia Road Books (www.ScotiaRoadBooks.com)

Detroit, Michigan

ISBN (paperback) 979-8-9876501-6-5

ISBN (epub) 979-8-9876501-7-2

Library of Congress Control Number: 2024924283

Interior by Scotia Road Books

Cover design by Susan Jones and Patrick McEntaggart

Printed in the United States of America

BLURBS

"Get swept away in the beauty of Lynne's writing, and the care in which she crafts each and every essay.

To write from the heart requires first baring your soul—a place of vulnerability that few authors have the strength, confidence, and ability to enter. Yet that is precisely what Lynne Golodner manages in *Forest Walk on a Friday*.

Do you value elegant writing, fresh storytelling, all penned by a writer who isn't hiding behind pretense or a carefully crafted avatar? A writer like you. A writer like me—broken, imperfect, and struggling in this complicated dance we call life. Then **I dare you to get swept away in the beauty of Lynne's writing**, and the care in which she crafts each and every word."

Danny Hankner, Editor-in-Chief & Founder, *Story Unlikely*

"This is **a beautiful collection of landscapes geographical and biographical**—from Michigan and Hawaii to Scotland and Budapest; Israel to India and back again. With reflections ranging across family, food, faith and more, Lynne Golodner excels at **capturing the messy reality of being human**: being a woman; being Jewish; being a parent; being a lover. And the exact tastes and textures of eating a tomato off the vine."

Elizabeth Gowing, prize-winning author of six books and co-founder of the Ideas Partnership

"Lynne Golodner's *Forest Walk on a Friday* is **an inspiring meditation that engages every one of the five senses.** It made me want to dig my hands in the earth, make chicken soup from scratch, climb a mountain, and then write about all of it.

Dancing with her Judaism as an Orthodox wife, a mother negotiating her children's relationship with religion, a post-October 7th witness and volunteer, and a tourist walking the streets of Budapest, Golodner explores God, privilege, and what it means to be at home and to be human.

Through the connected essays, we journey with Golodner as she discovers who she is and how she fits into the world she inhabits. A writer who is called to make meaning out of the mundane, **Golodner shows how to wonder, to recognize beauty, and to embrace life's glorious details**."

Jessica Fein, author of *Breath Taking: a memoir of family, dreams and broken genes*

"Lynne Golodner takes us on a journey of forging her path that **breathes meaning into life and bathes the soul**. In each of the lyrical and lush essays in *Forest Walk on a Friday*, Golodner weaves a tapestry of moments that includes riveting adventures, passionate introspection and often to destinations most have never known."

Kim Kozłowski, writer and *Detroit News* journalist

"Lynne Golodner's *Forest Walk on a Friday* is a significant addition to her enormous literary output. She has proven herself to be a popular and widely read novelist, essayist and poet. **She is one of Michigan's true renaissance writers.** This great collection of essays follows closely on the heels of her acclaimed novels, *Cave of Secrets* and *Woman of Valor*. In *Forest Walk*, Ms. Golodner shows us the depth and scope of her prose and of human emotions. She takes readers to a variety of places in these essays. From her experiences with Orthodox Judaism to interesting scenes in Scotland, Jerusalem, and India, there are insightful moments of motherhood, raising her children as a single mother, and family. She shows how she uses swimming as a meditation, and she offers a unique look at life and death through the passing of her beloved father. **This book has it all.** I was both intrigued and delighted to travel with this author wherever she took me. Her prose is descriptive, original and thoroughly engaging. Lynne's examination of her life through essays will be of interest to everyone. There are lessons here we all can learn from. I highly recommend this original book of experience and contemplation. The book is filled with experiences of joy, adventure and some sadness. *Forest Walk on a Friday* is well worth lacing up your hiking boots to follow along."

M. L. Liebler, author of *Hound Dog: A Poet's Memoir of Rock, Revolution and Redemption*

For Dan

I love going through life with you.

PUBLICATIONS

Sincerest thanks to these publications, where some of the essays in this collection first appeared:

45th Parallel

Abandon Journal

Adelaide Literary Magazine

bioStories

Consequence Forum

The Dillydoun Review

The Forward

The Good Life Review

Great Lakes Review

Green Golem Magazine

Hadassah Magazine

The Jewish Literary Journal

Midstory Magazine

Moment Magazine

Porridge Magazine

QuibbleLit

Story Unlikely
The Times of Israel
Valiant Scribe
Your Tango

BOOKS BY LYNNE GOLODNER

Fiction

I Love You, Charlie Tanner (May 2025)

Cave of Secrets

Woman of Valor

Poetry

Driving Off the Horizon (Lynne Cohn)

Living Inside: The Poetry of Prayer (Lynne Schreiber)

Nonfiction

The Flavors of Faith: Holy Breads

Stand Out from the Crowd: The Your People Guide to
Beside-the-Box, Funky, From-the-Heart, DIY Marketing,
PR & Social Media

Hide & Seek: Jewish Women and Hair Covering (Lynne
Schreiber)

In the Shadow of the Tree: A Therapeutic Writing Guide
for Children with Cancer (Lynne Schreiber)

Residential Architecture: Living Places (ghost-written for
Dominick Tringali)
A Patient's Guide to Understanding Cutaneous Lym-
phoma

CONTENTS

THE ROADS WE TRAVEL

1

THE ROADS WE TRAVEL

To be a religious Jew, one must pretend the outside world does not exist: burrow into a home infused with the scent of baking bread, meat and potatoes bubbling in a pot, husband and wife in separate beds, lights set to timers. In that structured life, everything focuses on the Sabbath: the days before devoted to planning and cooking and phone call invitations for celebratory meals, the days after filled with leftovers and cleaning. Husbands are commanded to satisfy their wives on the Sabbath. There are rules for everything: how and when to pray, which foods to eat and which to avoid, how much skin women can reveal (skirts four inches below the knee, sleeves past the elbow, clavicle covered), to shun clothing that mixes wool and linen. Married women hide their hair and never sing in front of men. The rabbis say the rules make it easier to reach God.

For the ten years I lived in that world, I thought it was

God I was reaching for.

***

With you, I wanted to abandon everything and drive, to love the meandering, adopt your freedom to just go. But you drove most of our miles while I dozed in the passenger seat.

Our love began when you parked your brown sedan in my driveway, and I took you to the mall to buy clothes you'd never wear. To please me, you bought pleated trousers and shiny button-downs, but in my memory, you're always wearing the frayed khakis, and I hate that I tried to change you.

You were the oldest person at the Dave Matthews concert in that big arena with its dirt floor and folding chairs. As Tim Reynolds played his saxophone, I closed my eyes and leaned my head back, your hand on my neck, your body shadowing mine, moving with the music. After, in my bed, night air sifting through the window screen, we took it slow. It sort of scared me, all your years lived when I was just beginning, your eclectic string of jobs perfect for a book cover bio: gas station attendant, harvesting farmhand, fisherman off the coast of Nova Scotia, journalist on three continents. You were in the process of divorcing a Jewish woman who wore long skirts and had soft curly hair, a lot like me, only I was 18 years younger. With me, you could pretend you were just beginning.

***

I need maps and directions, a destination, a purpose. I look for the quickest route between two places. Get me there sooner, faster. The journey cannot be my destination.

A drive from Seattle to Washington, D.C., bisects mountains and meadows on open stretches of highway. I knew someone once who traveled that route by bicycle just to see if he could. It took the whole summer, and he ended the trip exhausted and content, young and yearning. I could relate.

My first taste of Orthodoxy happened in Washington, on a Friday night in a friend's home. I watched two candles burn into memories, mesmerized by the dancing flames. My friend had been married to her childhood sweetheart for 20 years. They sang Hebrew and blessed their daughter in the waning day. They asked about my family and whether a life of Jewish rules could be enough for me. At their table, I started to consider living the way they did. Conversation lingered long into the night. The moon shone through the window in their guest room as I tried to sleep in the arc of its light, imagining walking to synagogue on Saturdays, noticing cracks in the pavement, eating kosher food, isolating from the fast-paced world, believing my lifestyle was God's intention, believing there was a God to direct all the people.

***

I first met you in New York, when I was a journalist fresh from college and you were the London editor. You breezed into the newsroom, the dashing man with a baritone like the deepest river, that wide smile behind the soft beard, brown eyes sparkling. You were kind and gentle from the first hello. A year later, when I worked in the Washington bureau and you were my boss in New York, I called you for advice or to complain, but really, I just wanted to hear your voice.

By the time we fell in love, I was freelancing in Michigan. I'd bought a house in a sleepy suburb, while your marriage was ending, your khakis roped together with a braided belt, cuffs shredding at the floor.

Our long, late-night calls and tender emails were a refuge from the insecurity of owning a house on a freelancer's income. I was so afraid I wouldn't make it. You drove 10 hours to me, and during the first furtive visits, we were all desire and yearning like a dreamscape in a movie. Your gentle hands quickening the beat of my heart, your honest interest in planting a garden and making a slow meal in my small kitchen.

I hated the games that boys played. You were solid, planted on the earth. Long past shaping your identity, you loved me as a memory of who you once were. You were older, still married, my former boss, so many reasons I wasn't supposed to love you, which is exactly why I did.

***

Were we always driving? Heading west, across patchwork highways, northern Indiana under the lip of Lake Michigan, smokestacks blanketing the lakeshore with tiny particles of dust. Through Chicago, to the flatlands of South Dakota, the Corn Palace, Wall Drug, the Badlands. We missed Mount Rushmore when your car broke down and waited for AAA to arrive. We sat on the side of the road, our feet dusty in the gravel, the still, white sky in a hot day and nothing to say because we'd said it all as the miles peeled away.

Looking back, I like to think the romance of the road entranced me. You were okay not knowing where we'd sleep each night. One late night, we passed the barbed wire of an Indian reservation and ended up at a Christian bed and breakfast. I found it comforting, so many conflicting identities in the same landscape, as if any one could be a wonderful choice.

You loved me with focused attention and quiet study. You introduced me to rutabaga, didn't judge me for eating Burger King, loved my hippie skirts and soft belly. We covered so many miles under the hot sun, soundtracked by conversation and music on the radio. I wanted to tell you everything, and you were content to listen. On those long stretches of endless road, you never felt the need to speak. Sometimes, I wanted your words, your no to my yes, your questions, your nuanced perspective. Your silence was meant to be supportive, even loving, but I wanted to scream just to hear a voice ricochet off the asphalt. I loved the distraction of our spontaneous turn-offs to walk onto a rugged landscape or make love because we could not wait for a destination.

If we had a fork in our road, it was the hike in the Big Horn Mountains. Your little car groaned into the steep incline that took us to the trailhead. I couldn't look over the edge outside the window—the drop was too severe, fear filling my throat. You took it slow, leaning into the mountain, and then we were on its back, in the forest, stepping over ribbons of knotted roots.

On that hike, I talked for an hour about why I loved an Orthodox Shabbat, describing the walk to synagogue beneath oak and maple trees, calling out *Good Shabbos* to people in dresses and suits, arriving at the home of an acquaintance with a bottle of wine. Hefting up the trail, you reached a hand to guide me over the rough terrain.

I wanted you to say you'd convert, promise to marry me and find a way to make meaning in the mundane. I wanted you to show me which path to take. Anything but silence, and in my head I raged, wanting to shake you awake. Was it because you knew I had to try everything, to have no regrets? Or did you know that no matter what you said, we were rest stops for each other on a long and winding road?

We climbed to an ice-cold lake and ate cheese and grapes while gazing at the sky. The Orthodox have blessings for every moment: a snack and a sunrise and a rainbow and the first time you see the ocean after a long time away from it. I wanted to consecrate that beautiful hike, but I didn't have the words. We could have prayed together, if I'd known how. You would have done anything I asked.

That night, tired and aching from the thousand feet we climbed, I clung to you at my friend David's house, listening to the river gulping outside the open window, his dogs barking to answer the howl of coyotes in the distance. I want to say we made love with the fierceness of two people destined for an intense farewell, to forever own the searing touch of your skin against mine. But all I can remember is the cool mountain breeze coming in the window and the constant sound of the river and your body beside mine radiating heat.

I had to be in Iowa by late July for a writers' conference, and so we pushed the little sedan hard to cover the miles in time. I pulled out my car-warm bags and kissed you then watched you fade into the distance, crying at the inevitability of our ending.

After you, I spent a decade with religion, married to a man who wore a yarmulke and with whom I birthed three babies. I thought the structure would suck me into black-and-white belonging, but I was made for bright color. By the time I left that world, you were married again, with a son of your own.

All my life, I've witnessed the streets wear away under traffic and winter salt and blowing sands and harsh storms. We are always rebuilding, widening, finding new ways to structure pavement to withstand greater loads. American highways are a foot thick and covered in asphalt or concrete, with sand and rock mixed in to strengthen the base. Everything needs fortification. Trucks trundle along the web of paths that crisscross our country, shaking its foundations with their heavy cargo. Sometimes, I wonder what used to stand where these roads are now, what had to come down for us to move forward.

This essay was first published in STORY UNLIKELY on July 5, 2022. https://mailchi.mp/93c53fecf2a6/story-unlikely-the-roads-we-travel?e=a30e32314f

2

— · —

CLIMBING DOG MOUNTAIN

Salmon swim upstream so their offspring will survive. Born in fresh water, they migrate to the ocean and return to seed a new generation. No small thing, the act is borne of pure instinct. They heft and push against the current until they find a little alcove where their eggs can grow.

I felt a kinship with those fish, fighting against the flow. A month divorced, alone on a mountaintop, I missed my three children, ages two, four and six, but needed to chart a new path for all of us. My marriage hadn't been horrible, but I'd known six weeks before we married that he was not right for me. I just didn't want to cancel the black-tie wedding and wait longer than age twenty-eight to find someone to marry. Now I had three children whom I loved more than anything. For the first week that I'd be away from them post-divorce, I ventured to the Pacific North-west, a place I'd never been, to celebrate my thirty-seventh birthday and explore mountains and valleys and the city of Portland to see if I could find wisdom in the landscape and, perhaps, a way forward.

Birds winged among white oak and ponderosa pine. Wind feathered through chocolate lily, woodland star and fairy slipper. I listened to the conversations of the trees, discovering the beauty in being alone.

I entered a meadow ablaze in wildflowers, sank to the ground and pulled just-picked strawberries from my pack. Far below me, the blue ribbon of the Columbia River snaked through the valley. I imagined salmon catapulting through it to spawn, water swelling around them as they surged against the current.

Dog Mountain starts at a base of 150 feet and rises to nearly 3,000 over three miles of trails, its summit overlooking the Columbia River Gorge. Six miles total of meandering through heavy forest and meadows and a former fire lookout. I had never hiked that far in one go, and I was wholly unprepared for the severity of this hike. I'd never even wandered trails alone. It was not easy for a flatlander from the Midwest, but I believed I could do it, so I huffed with the ascent, the forest growing thicker and darker, roots snaking across my path. I passed no one on the way up. Deep in the woods without cell service, I tried not to think about rattlesnakes and scorpions, steep slopes or slick paths, all the ways this blissful journey could go wrong. I wanted to find the waterfall through the tangle of trees and slip my feet into the cold water, but I could only hear its soothing rush somewhere far away.

***

My son Asher made his way into the world on a Friday afternoon in mid-March of my 30th year, when Michigan roads were icy and the air held a bite of cold. He did not cry, just looked around while a nurse weighed him. I would love him in ways that I longed to be loved. My 1970s parents did their best to love me as fully and completely as any parents love their children and spent more time with us than their parents lavished on them. But I felt like a fish out of water, like I didn't fit in my family. I withheld tears to avoid being called *too sensitive*. When I argued, I was called bossy, told I had a big mouth. I wanted to be appreciated for every inch of my rebellious self, to hear that my strident words and constant pushback showed strength and power and leadership and could be loved. But maybe that is too much to ask for any generation of parents; some are poised to handle the fragile flower of a feels-too-much kid, while others simply are not.

I wanted my children to know they were wonderful exactly as they are. They slept beside me, nursed and huddled in a sling while on the go. I believed these tiny souls needed to be close until they chose to separate, and I promised to pay attention and listen well.

Eliana was born when Asher was eighteen months old, and Shaya came two years after that. I cooked the meals, bought the clothes, did the laundry and organized the house while supporting my family by writing freelance articles for newspapers and magazines. My husband was playing at being a freelance musician who did not perform on Fridays or Saturdays due to his Orthodox Jewish religious observance. He was a night owl while I rose before the sun. Most nights, he languished in our basement, in front of the computer or on the phone, while I went to bed alone. We fought incessantly—about his being late for dinner (where had he been?), where the money disappeared to (he never could explain it), why he went to therapy three times a week and paid with a credit card when he generated no income. When Asher got recurrent ear infections, I feared his body was trying to shut out all our yelling.

A month after Shaya was born, my husband left for a week of unpaid gigs in Israel. I begged friends and family for advice. *Should I leave? What would life be like as a single mother? Would I ever find love?* Shaya lay across my lap as Eliana and Asher built forts out of blankets. When my husband called, the line crackled. His words cut in and out across the distance.

I thought about our 350-person wedding in a hotel ball-room, my handmade dress of pearls, sequins, creamy satin and sheer sleeves, our awkward, fumbling wedding night. The continuous voice in my head: *this doesn't feel right, there must be something better, why did I settle?* I wondered why he didn't see how hard it was to be alone with three small children, why he didn't choose to be by my side, why he didn't want me. Shouldn't we be in love with the family we created? Seven years in, shouldn't our marriage have turned into a deep and growing kind of love?

And then I remembered a moment at our wedding, when we were hoisted on chairs during the *hora*. He reached a white napkin out to me, a symbolic gesture re-calling more religious times when the bride and groom were not supposed to touch in public. He laughed and laughed, and I stared from my bouncing chair, gripping the arms so I wouldn't fall, wondering what was so funny. Later, he told me that he'd used the napkin to wipe sweat from his face before handing it to me. A symbolic gesture. A schoolyard joke. We were misaligned from the start.

An older friend said, "It's okay if you wait a year. You have a newborn and two toddlers. Give yourself time."

***

When Shaya was a year old, as a last attempt to save my marriage, I left Asher and Eliana with my parents and went to Aspen for a writers' conference with my husband and baby. As a freelancer working around the kids' naps and carpools, I wanted to expand editor relationships and perfect my craft. When I wasn't in workshops or at lectures, we hiked into the belly of Maroon Bells, Shaya on my husband's back, the silence of the mountains whispering around us.

I tried to find something to talk about, but nothing came except the *whoosh* of the wind. I stared into the distance as if the landscape held secrets. At night, all I wanted was to lie in bed with my baby and dream of the evergreens, the tiny dust clouds kicked up by my feet on the path, the view of clouds kissing mountaintops.

Back home, later that summer, my aunt and I traipsed along a hilly gravel road called Scenic Drive. In my sensitive, yearning childhood, my aunt had been my salvation. I'd call her for advice, support and reassurance that I was lovable. My mother's youngest sister, Auntie Suz is sixteen years older than me. When I was born, she drove around yelling out the open car windows, "I have a niece!" She was a hippie with long brown hair and bell-bottom jeans; at her wedding, I wore a yellow, ruffly flower girl dress and burst into tears under the *chuppah* because my new uncle was taking her away from me. When I turned ten, they took me for a camping weekend to celebrate my double-digits birthday.

As we hiked, I told her about my husband's five-figure therapy debt, his meager earnings from sporadic gigs. Squirrels scampered under trees. Thick bogs hid in dense woods. Birds and deer flitted in the shadows.

"He needs to find a therapist who takes insurance or go less frequently to this one," she said. "He needs to put the family first."

When I reiterated her words, my husband shook his head. Therapy would cure his depression and help him succeed as a musician, he insisted. "I'm not going less, and I'm not finding another therapist."

"Well, can you get a job to pay for therapy?"

"I can try," he said.

I looked at his blond goatee sprinkled with gray, his bald head which had been a downy crown when I first married him, the underbite his mother apologized for never correcting with braces. It's funny how a person can be attractive when you want them and not attractive whatsoever when they fall out of favor. I thought about how depressed he'd been when we met. He'd worn shorts with untucked T-shirts and unbuttoned flannels. I'd known we were not a perfect match but pledged to go through with the black-tie wedding because I believed I could help him become a better version of himself. I also hadn't believed I'd find someone better. Over the years, I'd gained confidence, which led me to feel I'd rather be alone than with the wrong man.

The light from a white sun bore through the window. My breath was even, my heartbeat calm as sleep. Being alone would be simpler, at least, and strengthening at best. That day, I renamed Scenic Drive the Freedom Trail.

He cried when I said I was leaving. "Will we be friends with benefits?" he asked as we divvied up the dishes.

I thought of the awkward nights when I wanted him to know my body but arched in discomfort when he touched me. For years, I'd dreamed of my college boyfriend and our easy passion, waking lonely beside my husband.

"You've got to be joking," I said.

***

When I hike, I wonder who chooses to map the mountain, to make paths in the wild, to determine where people should walk that won't hurt the forest. Someone tames the wilderness, to invite in those who want to learn its secrets. It feels brave, daring, to do such work.

In Michigan, there are woods with winding paths and some incline, but they're hills, not mountains. I needed a steep trail to feel the burn in my thighs and the heartbeat in my ears.

For so long, I'd relied on others for guidance. No one suggested listening to my own voice or making decisions on gut instinct. When I was a new mother, I scoured books for wisdom, but all the conflicting advice convinced me that only I could know what was best for my babies. I breastfed, co-slept, made chicken soup with sweet potato, zucchini and carrot, let them jump in puddles after a spring rain and whispered stories as they drifted to sleep. I created my parenting map, my instincts leading the way. Now I needed a map for myself.

***

I came to Dog Mountain on the recommendation of the hotel reception staff. Hipsters with piercings and man-buns, they'd asked whether I wanted an easy hike or a difficult one. I told them I was from the Midwest but up for a challenge. They said to pack plenty of water.

The hike is not just about exercise or pretty views. It's a

test of wills, an endurance feat, a challenge to see if I can be on this mottled dirt, at this moment, as the wind whips my hair around my face. It's an experiment to see if I can quiet my clanging mind, forget about all the moments I climbed over to find this spot, banish my fears about what lies ahead.

The descent is always faster than the climb, and easier. On Dog Mountain, there were more signs on the way down and lots of people. We exchanged smiles, strangers on a shared mission.

The hike consumed the whole of the day, and I returned exhausted but exhilarated, my curls plastered to my face, dirt in the creases of my eyes. I approached the reception desk as they were finishing their shift.

One of the guys looked at me and chuckled.

"Not sure I would have gone if you had told me how hard it was," I said.

"That's why we didn't tell you," he said.

After my divorce, a grueling hike became the easiest thing I could do. On the trail, there is nowhere to go but straight ahead. When I reached the top and started to head back down, I was reassured by the crisp air and waving branches. My body throbbed with the intensity of the forest and the excitement of my unclear future.

This essay first appeared in YOUR TANGO on June

*18, 2022, https://www.yourtango.com/self/climbing-dog-m
ountain-after-divorce-grueling-hike-easiest-thing-could-do*

3

— · —

LIVING WATERS

The black-glass water of Loch Garve reflected the slate of these Scottish mountains. On our way to Skye, no time to record the moments. Two and a half hours to get to that big place, and I wanted to see it all, to know the land, but every place is bigger than we think.

What does it mean to know a place, really? Is it the self that becomes known in a foreign landscape, and that's the best I could hope for?

And then there we were, at the base of steep green slopes, the mirror-glare of water spilling from far peaks. We bathed in the spray of waterfalls, meditated to the rush-and-crash of water on its way.

Near the Sligachan Old Bridge, the intersection buzzed with traffic, and my love and I stopped for a moment. The stone bridge arched over a slow-moving river of dark water from the Cuillin Mountains. Some say the waters are enchanted.

Decades earlier, in university, I'd read about Cú Chulainn but couldn't penetrate the old words. Didn't have the patience, then, to relate to legend. At fifty-one, though, the story of a battle involving Scotland's fiercest female warrior, Scáthach, gripped me. A strong woman, canonized. And her daughter weeping by the Sligachan River, pleading for the conflict to end. Children carry the wounds of their elders, generational trauma. They become our salvation, finding resolution where we cannot.

Once, the water was a gateway between human and fairy. The fairies told the crying girl to dunk her head for seven seconds, and she'd surface knowing how to save her mother.

Did it work? I have no way of knowing. But people seek out this bridge, where the wind screams and the water never stops. They kneel at the river's edge, hold their breath and plunge their faces into the icy water. Counting to seven, they expect to emerge with a beauty that never fades. I suppose that's a kind of wisdom.

The ground is soft with mud and moss, bouncy under foot. My hair whips around my face. I knot it, but it breaks free. I can't hear my husband's voice over the wind, so we walk wordless on uneven ground, climb down grassy hills to where the water pools.

"Dunk?" he asks.

I shake my head. I'm not searching for the superficial or longing to live forever. Growing old is a privilege, *better than the alternative*, my father always said. It's not always better or easier when we're young.

I finger the faint lines around my mouth, run a hand over my soft belly, grip the hips that brought three babies into the cold world. My body is well-earned, fully lived.

I dip my hand in the water, though, just to feel it: the kind of cold that is a form of honesty. A cold that makes you notice a moment and be thankful to draw breath.

4

—·—

STILL, THE DANDELIONS COME

They grew up and out, gripping the soil, fanning in circles of soft jagged leaves like neck ruffles on Victorian royalty. Perfectly symmetrical, actually beautiful. Like art. Some small, some large, ready for picking, for cooking, for fermenting. But we don't eat dandelions from the yard, though I'll buy them from the farmers market in a bunch, cleaned and beautiful in their feather lightness and elegant length. At home, we only harvest what we choose to grow, not what pushes through on its own, in spite of us.

Perhaps it's a modern mindset that limits my perspective. I was not raised to forage for my survival, to learn local plants and cultivate what comes easily or within reach. Dandelions litter the garden. Every year, all season long, I pull them out, toss them in a lawn bag for disposal. But why? They grow and they grow, offering vitamins, nutrients and perennial goodness, just for me to hack them out, rejecting their simple, easy offering.

Last Mother's Day, my daughter Eliana said we should do something together to celebrate, like a forest hike. I wanted to dig up the grass and double the size of my garden. "Help me dig," I said.

She put on flimsy white tennis shoes and jumped on the edge of a shovel to push it into the hard ground. "I'm only doing this because it's Mother's Day," she said, sweat glistening along her temples.

The dandelions, bright green and hardy, grew up through the toughest corners—where concrete paving blocks lay next to an electrical outlet, in the crevices between garden and grass. They had grit and endurance, bursting through hard earth, clinging to soil, reluctant to be removed. My shovel could only attack at certain angles.

Taraxacum, the genus known more generally as the dandelion, is one of the most common plants in the world, edible in its entirety, from yellow flower down to the hard roots. One of the most vital early spring sources of nectar for pollinators, dispersing over great distances, carried on the wind.

"Why don't we eat them?" Eliana asked. "Why not these?"

I dropped the fans of leaves into a paper bag, searching for a good answer. So this fall, when I pulled up the garden to prepare the earth for winter, I gazed at the newest dandelions—so many symmetrical leaves, artful in their points and right-angled cuts along each narrowing shaft—and wondered why I work so hard to throw them away.

In fifth grade at Forest Elementary School, classes suspended for field day. It was brisk spring, when the air has a nip but the ground is thawing and a gray sky promises future sun. My frizzy hair pulled into pigtails, my jeans with rolled cuffs because my mother refused to shorten them as I'd just grow taller. We had two days off classes and lots of events to compete in and learn about the natural world—foot races and forest walks and art projects involving leaves and thick paper. I was in a group tasked with making dandelion salad. "You can eat them," a teacher said, but I didn't believe her.

Scientists say dandelions evolved over more than 30 million years, and humans have consumed them for a long time—as nutrition, as medicine, as a healing tea, in traditional Chinese medicine and in the Native American palate.

We set off along the sloping field and into the adjacent forest as well as into the yards of houses that bordered the school grounds. And when we pulled the dandelions from the hard earth, the teacher tore the leaves the same way my mother shredded lettuce and tossed it in a bowl to drizzle with oil and vinegar and sprinkle salt over top. "Good enough to eat," she said, and I tasted them and was surprised by the tang and the bite.

This fall, it took all of a day to pull out everything growing in my garden. Nine tomato plants thick at the base and deep in the soil, stalks reaching in all directions. Some leaves had started to brown, and hard green orbs clung to the branches but refused to ripen. I bent the branches to fit them into bags, tossing metal cages onto the grass to organize later. I raked the soil smooth for the coming slumber of winter.

The raw greens are rich with vitamins A, C and K, calcium, potassium, iron, manganese and lutein. The flowers contain phytochemicals including polyphenols, and the roots offer inulin. Every piece of the plant has value, from the seeds floating through the neighborhood to the roots which can be roasted into a coffee alternative.

I had crowded in so many plants that the cucumber vines snaked through the garden, choking the eggplant, which didn't grow to full height until late August, after the cucumbers turned yellow and withered. I pulled at long vines of rotted vegetables, reeling them into the trash. Too late, I noticed two budding zucchinis, which might have grown fatter before the last warm day if I had left them.

Spotting one budding eggplant, I left the soft leaves and lavender flowers, hoping the last few warm days of full sun would sprout new fruit before the frost. I left the lavender, too, which neither grew bigger nor shrank all summer, and hoped it might weather our harsh, gray winters and become a perennial with promise. I doused the banana plant near the hedge, hoping it might live through the cold and bloom.

Once, I drank dandelion wine in an Amish village somewhere on the road between home and away, with an older lover. I was in my twenties, eager to wander and explore. The wine was syrupy thick, too sweet, even then, when sugar was magnetic.

When I married the first time, we bought into a farm share that delivered a box of produce every week of the growing season. I learned to cook the bitter greens of beets and bake them into a pie with cheese and eggs. And one day, long after that marriage ended, I started buying long, clean dandelion leaves bound together with a rubber band at the farmers market. It never occurred to me to cull them from my yard, from the rich soil of my garden. I cooked them in a skillet with olive oil, garlic, salt and the juice of half a lemon. Sometimes, I zested lemon peel over top. The kids never liked the bitterness, but I felt like I was returning to some hidden part of myself, close to the land

and unafraid of what grows near my home.

Found on six continents and part of virtually every menu in history, it grows back despite all efforts to kill it.

But come fall, I return to habit, digging out pernicious weeds, persistent plants that refuse to give over control. Even as I wrested them free of the cloying ground, digging until my hand closed around the hard white roots, I wanted to double-back, to give them their due, show respect for the hardiest among us.

The next week, three deer came, a doe and two fawns. Their graceful heads bobbed—we'd let the grass be overtaken by wild strawberry and clover, a fine meal for wild mammals. They munched at the bushes and trees, pulling leaves between their teeth. When I stepped outside, the mother deer lay on the ground, flanks folded beneath her, ears alert and twitching. She stared at me, and I backed into the house.

"You win," I said.

For hours, she lounged on my ground, nibbling. After five, my husband came home. The doe watched, listened. When his car lumbered into the garage, when the door lifted with a thunderous thwack-thwack, her ears twitched and she tensed at our soft steps, at the swish of his car door closing. I waved for him to follow me into the yard.

"You've had long enough," I said. She stood, staring

right at me, daring me closer.

Dan flapped his arms. "Go on now," he called.

We stepped deeper into the yard, peered around the back of the brick garage, where her fawns stood, watching, waiting for their mother's lead. The banana plant had withered and shrunk into itself, the ends of the leaves nibbled to nubs. The mother leaped over the back fence, and the babies followed. I could see the outline of the mother's ribs through her fur. I had left her alone all day to make use of what is abundant. Somebody should. Animals know.

It's a good day when I play in the yard. This year, everything burst forth under the rainbow spray of cold water, under blazing sun, under varying days when I couldn't tell what season was really upon us.

When I moved into this house, the backyard was littered with debris. Fallen trees, heaps of dead leaves and at its center, an overgrown sculpted hedge surrounded by thorny roses, pretty things with no purpose, and the refuse of a yard growing in on itself. Our children were little, so we pulled out the thorny plants and hacked the bushes to the ground, feeding the soil and erecting a fence so we could plant vegetables and keep pests away. There are rats in this neighborhood, but I've never seen them, though raccoons, possum, chipmunks and squirrels abound.

Year after year, I plant the garden and bask in the glory

of budding fruit and sprouting leaves. My hands press the damp soil, and I breathe in the heady scent of all that is natural. I think I am cultivating nourishment, but really, the world has a way of regenerating itself despite me.

I pull at what we call weeds, pests, reverting to the bias of my youth. A weed is a "plant not valued for use or beauty," but everything has a purpose. My fifth-grade teacher tried to tell me that we could live on what grows wild, but I was raised to believe in store-bought and pre-packaged.

The other day, I wondered if I could sit beside the deer and have a conversation. I'd like to talk with someone who just knows in her body how to live in this world.

This essay was first published in 45TH PARALLEL on June 1, 2023, https://issuu.com/45thparallelmag/docs/45th _parallel_magazine_2.3

5

FOREST WALK ON A FRIDAY

New grass, wet from the night, under a sky the blue of a baby blanket. The sun is hot and white, glittering the dewy grasses. An airplane thunders overhead. Far traffic is a river rushing.

I hide in the cool shadow of a Norway spruce. So many critters hiding in the open. Birds loud and constant, each call different, sound and purpose.

The trees have yet to awaken, but at home, the pink buds of a magnolia have burst forth and the daffodils are full-throated.

Every time I come to the forest, it's different, but so am I. In past Aprils, I've stepped over black and white banded snakes coiling around each other. Today, I can't even find the holes they slither into.

Feather dusters of pine branches carpet the velvet ground. I follow the River Trail to the bridge, which has new, chest-height railings, the metal rusted from winter.

The brown river eddies under low branches. A deer in the shallows tugs at leaves. A mate on the hill starts at a man's voice. *Shhh, quiet.* What is there to say in the forest? A third doe steps into the brush, her fan-like ears cocked, her muzzle tilting to the edible. Hooves crunching over matted ground, her black eyes lock on me, and she canters into the water, crosses to dry ground. In a moment, their brown-gray bodies disappear into the sleeping trees.

I walk on. My breathing thickens, my heart pulsing in my temples, the rat-a-tat-tat of a woodpecker echoing. I go-go-go up the matted hill, thinking only about how hard it is and how far I have to go. Another plane hums overhead, a fly buzzes, circling. The air smells warm.

Skunk cabbage leaves like vulvas are coming up from the ground, soft and satin, favoring the black, water-soaked soil. One of the first spring-blooming plants, changing constantly as the year unfolds, at its heartiest, *symplocarpus foetidus* reaches nearly three feet across with giant green leaves.

I finish the River Loop, the brown ribbon sparkling in the morning sun. The streams should be pulsing with runoff, but they are slow and trickling. I've been here in winter when ice cracked over black water and deer left deep prints in the snow. Then, the sun was blinding in a different way, and I could not discern between the deep cold of the season and my organic heat.

A fly alights on my page, its bulbous green body like satin. I trace its outline with my gaze, but then it lifts off and away. Back on the bridge, I can't spot the deer anywhere. I take the main trail back to where I began. This ground, flat and solid, packed in over millennia, holds me, supports me, allows me to join the knowing journey of all that lives and answers to itself.

There is activity among the trees—skittering, rustling, shuffling under ground cover, hiding in shadows—but the forest shows only what it wants me to see, never quiet, never still, living its purpose without the drag of thought or wondering.

A child clomps over a distant trail and screams. I hear him but can't see him. When I was a child, no one brought me to the forest, but I took my children there again and again so they would never be afraid of the naked and bold world.

This essay was first published in ABANDON JOUR-NAL on May 6, 2024. https://abandonjournal.com/lynne-golodner/forest-walk-on-a-friday/

6

FLEETING, LIKE THE DRAGONFLY

The first moments in the kayak: *I can't believe I get to part these waters, spend my day floating down a river.* Trees lean into the eddies; shimmering fish waggle beneath the surface. My paddle dips in, water swirls, and I pull the boat forward. On logs, turtles are sunning their hard shells.

Insects ripple the surface of the river. When dragonflies hover, I paddle quietly, delicately, to not disturb them. Sometimes they fly while in the act of coupling, one on another as they flutter their wings and land on my craft, and I do everything I can to peel smoothly through the water, so they, and I, stay focused on the action of their lives.

No one told me exactly how a human life should unfold. The messages were subtle, not spoken. No words directed me to *go to school, get a job, buy a house you can't quite afford, make payments on everything you believe you own but never do, live for the sole purpose of working all the years of your life, until one day, you stop from a heart attack or a cancer diagnosis or just fall down too tired to get up again.* Implicit in the urge to *get good grades* and *make friends* was a lesson to follow the crowd, do as I see others doing. Don't question. Don't wonder. Live to work instead of working to live.

But that advice didn't sit well, so I cherish days on the river, where I settle the boat flat, swipe the tongue of the paddle into the river to power forward. When it all gets to be too much, I go to the water. A muddy stream, a lapping river, rolling lakes. Sun sparkling off ever-moving waves of perspective.

Having no color of its own, water merely reflects what hovers above or lies below. Bright blue from an endless sky. Murky gray from dusting swirls of a sandy bottom. Its story comes from everything it intersects with: plants and sky, soil and sand, green trees searing toward drifting clouds. All the concerns I bring to its shores float away like the dragonfly, in concert with the trickle of waves tripping over themselves. The symphony of living, the very definition of nature, where instinct takes over.

Is it no wonder, then, that dragonflies symbolize spiritual insight? They are the only creature that can see the full picture, 360 degrees all around. Every direction, taking in all at once. If only I could see it all as clearly, above the translucent water, a foil for my musings, a reflection for my wandering.

Dragonflies can spend four years as nymphs, shedding their skin again and again, until they transform into adults and go about their business of reproduction. Once they mate, they will die. This is their culmination. Every moment has led to this. Do they know the end is near? Does it matter? Perhaps their beauty comes from doing what they must, through the stages of life, taking what comes until it's over.

I dip my hand into the swift and consistent current. The water is cool, not cold, clear, but I cannot see to the depths. Besides, the bottom always looks closer than it is. The not knowing is soothing. Perhaps it's why I come.

On the river, I find a confluence of effort and ease. I push the water to propel myself forward, knowing it carries me and if I were content enough to just sit and glide, I would reach my destination eventually. I like to believe I have a role in my progress, but I'm not sure I do.

When I kayak with my husband, he mentions how fiercely I power each stroke to get down the river. "If they say it'll take three hours, it will take us two," he laughs. Hearing the words between his words, I dangle the paddle, wait before swiping it to pull the river along. He reminds me to be here, now, instead of racing to an inevitable finish.

The human goes through stages like the dragonfly, rushing from here to there: the child wants to grow up, the adult wants to revert to easier times. Human nature avoids settling in to the now. Even long-awaited retirement comes with trepidation for then we know the end is near.

Every summer, I paddle the Huron River, somewhere along its 130 miles, after it rises from a swamp in Springfield Township and long before it spills into Lake Erie. With its typical Midwest mudbanks, slow flow and low gradient, this river has twenty-four major tributaries, which adds 370 miles to its footprint. Supposedly named for the indigenous people who used to live around it, Huron is not a native name, only what the white men called the people who first claimed this place, who called the river something else, *cos-scut-e-nong sebee* or *Giwitatig-weisaibi*, words whose meanings have been lost.

The legacy of place gets muddied when I plumb through its history. The people we call native were not. They were pushed from their original home, forced to migrate south, carrying an old history on their backs. I come from an ancient people who walked through an uncertain desert for too many years. All of us can trace back to nomadic origins if we try. Regardless, we all migrated to the banks of a healthy river or a deep lake, water promising survival. Do I imagine the river saves me now, the moving waters a baptism, a new beginning?

For all the naming and claiming, the river marches on in spite of us. It grows, it dies, it refurbishes itself and we come to it seeking salvation, peace, expression, release. It seeps into its banks and flows along its course no matter what we call it or who claims it or who we shove out of its reach. It continues on long after we are gone.

There dances the dragonfly, stunning in its symmetry: translucent wings, brilliant blue head, iridescent body. Light as air. I only ever see them on the river, my face to the sun, the vast sky cast in white. It's as if in my desk-bound life, sealed between sturdy, cool walls, dragonflies are mythical creatures, bound only for stories and dreams. But I know that we inhabit the same landscape.

Somewhere beyond the golf course and the paved streets and the honking traffic, dragonflies go about their business of living. So small as to fit onto the eye of a pin, the dragonfly brain probably does not have the capacity to ponder the meaning of its existence, and that may be a gift. For the minute we start to wonder, we stop seeing, stop trusting the current, stop letting the river carry us along.

This essay was first published in GREAT LAKES RE-VIEW on February 23, 2023. https://greatlakesreview.org

/fleeting-dragonfly/

7

SWIMMING: A MEDITATION

When I was little, I rode on my father's back while he swam the length of our neighbor's pool in one breath. My legs gripping his sides, my arms waving in the wind, I tilted my head back and laughed as he pulled me through the water. The pool seemed impossibly long, and I could not imagine holding my breath the whole distance the way my father did. He carried me from the depths to the shallows, where I climbed off and he rose out of the water like a great whale's tail, shaking drops from his face, his grin as wide as mine. I believed he could do anything.

Four years ago, after my father was diagnosed with an incurable blood cancer, I sought the pool as refuge. When I sat at home on the couch, silent tears trailed down my face and I shuddered into the angsty anticipation of a world without him. In the pool, I couldn't cry. Once, tears overcame me in the middle of a swim, and I fought to breathe, stopping mid-lane and treading water to regain control. Crying ruined my rhythm and made me choke on chlorine, and I lost count of how many laps I'd completed.

My father swam backstroke at Mumford High School in the 1950s. One year for Halloween, I wore his robin's egg blue and burgundy varsity sweater, and all the parents smiled when they saw me, sharing memories as they dropped candy into my plastic pumpkin. I didn't think about my dad as an athletic star until he was dying though, when we had long conversations in his hospital room about the places he'd been and the things he'd accomplished. We hadn't swum together in years and we no longer could (with the port in his chest for infusions, a public pool could have killed him), so I settled for collecting his stories.

***

I've always found water soothing—being by its side, watching its tempestuous emotions, immersing in its cold embrace. The big gusty gales of Lake Michigan. The swift current of the Detroit River. The mirror-like surface of my next-door neighbor's pool, ready to absorb our summertime squeals and childhood energy. The ocean more powerful than what I imagine God to be, its strong hands reaching up and out, slapping the sand and peacefully retreating. Our bodies are mostly water, even our bones. We need water to survive, and in a way, it needs us too. We begin floating, and throughout our lives water symbolizes purity, fertility, life and renewal. But equally as much, water has long been a symbol of wisdom, power, grace. Essential for existence and cleansing, water has the power to change us and to bless. Some ancient cultures saw water as chaos, but I see it as deliverance. As much as its power can overwhelm, it gives me power that I desperately need.

Water is beautiful. Its movements, its elegant glow, its translucency, the rainbows it inspires when interacting with light at the right angles. I love to watch a raindrop on a blade of grass or a river cascade over rocks. I love the sound of water. I love the way it feels when I am in it, the way it holds me, allows me to be lighter than I am on land.

But I didn't always seek reassurance in the waves. I am not a lifelong competitive swimmer, nor a person home-birthed into a tub. I come from very mundane and ordinary roots. The pool only became my refuge when I was divorcing the father of my three children who were aged four, three, and one at the time. My work was imploding—the economic downturn caused so many of the magazines I had been writing for to halt publication or shutter completely. I went from earning six-figures as a freelance writer to desperately searching for people to hire me to write for a few hundred dollars at a time. And I wouldn't be getting much from my soon-to-be ex-husband, an Orthodox Jewish musician whose earning potential was limited because his faith prevented him from performing on Fridays and Saturdays.

A week after we signed the divorce judgment, my ex moved his boxes and suitcases out of our house. I sat on the carpeted steps while my kids watched *Sesame Street* in the family room. The big house was all mine, with its stone façade and two-car garage, my daughter's pink bedroom, the 1960s blue-tiled bathroom, the oak-floored living room, the 1980s kitchen with Formica counters and laminate cabinets, the basement that flooded in a hard rain. We had bought it at the height of the market, and now at the housing industry's lowest point, I couldn't even sell the house to pocket the proceeds. I was stuck with a mortgage to pay, lights and heat to keep on, a refrigerator to fill. For months, hoping to leverage my skills into a career pivot, I'd been looking for companies to hire me to write press releases and blogs. Some had signed on, but the CEO of my biggest client, a family-owned grocery chain, said my business idea was stupid. I wondered how I was going to make it.

Months later, when I had three clients and income to cover the mortgage and utilities, I scraped together enough money to join a health club with outdoor and indoor pools. Many afternoons I took the kids to the club, leaving them in childcare for an hour so I could swim laps alone then picking them up and swimming with them until they grew tired under the sun. The laps grounded me and reminded me to breathe, assured me that I could float in choppy waters. The time splashing with my children in the zero-edge kiddie pool showed me that I could work hard and have time to play. We would keep each other afloat. Those sun-lit days playing in the water with my children, I felt lucky. I was forging a path for us, and I even had time and space for fun on a hot day. Once, as we carried buckets and pool toys and bottles of sunscreen from the car to the club, my older son Asher asked why I had to swim alone before we could all swim together. I couldn't tell him that if I didn't swim, I might crumble in front of him. Instead I said, "It makes me a happier mommy,"and that answer seemed to suffice.

***

I never worried about money until I became a single mother. Then, I needed a safe car large enough for three car seats, clothing, winter coats, and sturdy boots for my children. They outgrew everything within months, and their hearty appetites demanded three nutritious meals a day, plus snacks, and sippy cups full of juice. One day in the not-so-distant future, they would need thick textbooks, sports equipment, SAT tutors, college tuition.

The money was a literal need, but it became a symbolic one too, representing my value, my success. No matter how much clients paid me, it was never enough for me to feel secure. In the year after the divorce, the notion of enough grew big and scary, a monster in the night looming over me as I tossed in bed. I called my father at least once a week asking for advice and seeking reassurance that I would land enough clients, that I could keep them. My father had created a company when I was ten. At the time he had three young children too, but my mother stayed home to raise us so he could go out and build a name for himself in the scrap metal industry. I had no fallback, no one to keep the homefront going while I went out into the world.

"Take the money and do the work," he said. "It'll all workout." A simple truth, that if I completed the work in front of me, I'd always have work to do. His advice was tangible and immediate. A job well done was the best way to ensure more jobs. Focusing on an unknown future took me out of the moment and away from delivering on any project. It tied me in knots I had a hard time climbing free from.

I loved the sound of my father's voice when he answered the phone and realized it was me: "Hi, Lynnie!" he'd exclaim, as if my call was a highlight of his day. It certainly was for me. He didn't say much about the specifics of my fears, just reassured me that if I kept showing up and doing well, I'd be okay. He never worried, and his voice calmed me, like the undulating waves of the pool do now. After he was diagnosed, I started saving his messages so I could listen to him long after he was gone.

***

My company grew and I gained more clients, developing a niche in the yoga world, where I helped studios and yoga personalities build brands, land TV interviews, and create social media content. Before I made the pool my sanctuary, under the guidance of one of my clients, I tried mindfulness meditation. I bought a Back Jack chair to put on the floor and left my desk twice a day to close my eyes and breathe in and out through my nose. I'd stare at the place where my third eye was supposed to be, trying to escape the papers cluttered around my computer, the oversight my employees required and the ongoing worry of whether I could retain clients while trying to attract more.

Meditation worked for a while. I grew calmer about managing my small staff and less concerned about money. But I fell out of practice. In the midst of work and home, too many demands competed for attention. I had to leave the scene of chaos to step into calm.

In a Michigan winter, it takes effort to drive icy roads, face the biting wind, peel off my clothes, and plunge into waiting waters. But still, I go. On a busy day, when there are more demands than minutes to devote to them, I go. When my children pull at me, beg me to sit with them on the couch, I promise to sit later, after I swim. The water beckons, and I respond. My anchor, my sustenance.

I love the equanimity of swimming. The water welcomes me, like a lover, and I give myself over to its embrace. For the first fifteen laps, worries clutter my mind, shouting: *my contract might be threatened, that client isn't happy, will any publication take my writing? Tick-tick-tick*: looming deadlines and endless to-dos. Soon, they will leave and silence will settle in, the rhythm of my body in the water, the peace of the pace. With every stroke, I am reaching for the inevitable calm.

I fill my lungs and push off from the wall. I part the waters, my legs fluttering. My hands are cups filling and emptying. I point my toes and tap my heels to complete a stroke. *There's no place like the pool.* Focusing on form lets the worries bubble up and float away. I breathe out of my nose, my skin pulses.

In breaststroke, my arms extend like eagle's wings before coming together at my heart and pushing forward. Backstroke and freestyle are long-limbed and reaching, exposing the heart. Even butterfly, which I rarely swim, is an open-arm hug before an elegant crashing into the water. In swimming I become expansive, open to everything, full of love for this moment, full of understanding for all the complications in and around me. I become an observer, not a judge.

***

In high school, swim class was mandatory for ninth graders. The gym teacher handed out brown, starchy swimsuits that were washed every night in abrasive industrial detergent. We clipped the straps together with a barrette to keep them from falling down. When my oldest son Asher was in high school, he swam against my alma mater, and my mother, father, and I watched from the bleachers. The pool seemed half the size it was in the 1980s. In my memory I treaded water, staring up at bleachers that rose like mountains of creaking seats the gym teacher traversed, shouting instructions. Asher was not a fast swimmer, but he took whatever the coach threw at him. Once, forced into the 500, the longest and hardest event in the competition, he finished last. I watched with a knotted stomach, nervous that all eyes were on my boy. I admired his resolve to plow through one lap at a time, as if no one were there, immersed in the water's lulling support. The natatorium shimmered with cheering. After, he and my dad commiserated about what it felt like to compete in the pool. Although all eyes were on them, they lost themselves in the rhythm of the strokes. It was as if the rest of the world fell away. I knew exactly what they meant.

***

With every length, my worries have less energy and I have more. Twenty lengths in, my mind quiets. Until I reach my rhythm, I negotiate with myself to keep going: *Another ten lengths. If you want to quit at thirty, fine.* But I never quit. Once I am submerged, I stay. After thirty lengths, it's all freestyle, long and gliding. Worries are little birds flying away without sound. *Safe travels, little creatures—go find light and warmth.*

***

I spent two years watching my father die. When his life finally ended on a dark, windy day, I thought, *I spend my life waiting, and then death comes to the door. There is no better time for anything.*

I'd been wanting to visit the Keys for years. I yearned to leave the gray cold, short days and ice-crusted streets for slow beach strolls, an unlimited horizon and the cool reassurance of a shimmering pool, a kiss of sweet air on my skin. I drove lonely, two-lane roads under bright sun, crossing long and narrow bridges stringing islands together until I arrived in the tropical refuge of a seaside resort. I chose Cheeca Lodge in Islamorada because it had a lap pool. I could swim in the milky dawn counting lengths by the clicking of insects.

Breathing in the winter can be painful—each inhale burns and harsh wind bites exposed skin, turning it red and raw. I needed to be in a place where it didn't hurt to breathe, where I could bare my skin and feel the sun seep in quietly, kindly. It was more than a literal winter that February. The weeks after my father died were the darkest time of my life.

I loved those early mornings flip-flopping across asphalt, past the golf course where sprinklers *switch-switch-switched,* all peaceful silence and reverence for the rising day. The air was cool, like the water. I was the only one in the pool that early, the morning whispering reassurances like my father used to. With each lap, I felt more certain that I could continue on without him, even if I didn't want to.

***

The water and I, we are close. I push and it pushes me back. I glide and it holds me. It molds around my body, and I let it comfort me. I breathe out as long as I can until there is no air left. I am a buoy in a constant current. I cannot sink no matter how hard I try.

When I finish the longest part of my set, steam rises from my skin, and I duck under to cool my face. The drumbeat of music in the speakers is as rhythmic as the waves. I can't make out words, and I don't really want to. Children squeal and splash, old people float in the shallows, a marathoner in the next lane pounds up and down the lane. Everything is happening around me, and the worries I brought to the pool have long since floated away. Everything that felt heavy, draining, is simple in the haze from the water. The world is an unimportant blur.

My main set done, I proceed through my last twenty-two lengths to hit my mile. I alternate strokes, slow my pace. In my water cocoon, I watch bubbles become blinking stars in a night sky.

I've swum three or four times a week for more than a decade now, and I sought refuge in a pool long before that. But only in the past few years have I realized that, in the pool, I find the comfort and support my father gave me. Swimming infuses me with strength, clarity and determination like my conversations with Dad. I no longer need to hear his words to know everything will be alright. In the absence of his voice, I listen to my own.

I finish every swim with side stroke, a kindness to my weary self. Goggles off, I lay my head in the water as if it is my father's palm. My hands and legs scissor in opposite directions. Water gurgles in my ear. And when I rise from the pool, sparkling drops drip off of me, my hair shaking out from its cap molding. I am the great whale's tail, inhabiting the space my father used to occupy with his single-breath strength—I am carrying the little girl to safety.

This essay was first published in THE GOOD LIFE REVIEW on February 5, 2022, https://thegoodlifereview.com/issue-six/6-nonfiction/swimming-a-meditation-by-lynne-golodner/

8

WHEREVER I GO, I AM HOME

1983, Farmington Hills, Michigan

Ian lived on the other side of the creek. Past the tall grasses at the edge of the yard, bordered by the bike path and the wooden bridge that crossed a creek where minnows wagged through a trickle of water. When he moved in after sixth grade, we became immediate best friends. But I was not allowed to phone him—my parents believed girls calling boys was "chasing," so I had to wait for his call every day after school. It came without fail, and I sat on my bed with the pastel comforter, leaning into the beige genie phone. We talked for an hour, sometimes longer. Once, I opened my bedroom window and he stood a stereo speaker in his living room window and played a favorite song across the open field for me to hear.

In the summer, the heat was blinding and still. Ian and other boys played football in the field behind my house, sweaty in the long grass. I watched them, listened to their shouting, their feet tromping, the thud of bodies colliding.

Once, my father planted apple trees in our backyard. We waited five years for fruit to appear. Manicured lawn ended in wild grasses under a hot sun. A common area meandered through the center of the neighborhood. The air whistled through the spokes of my bicycle wheels as I pedaled on paths and over wooden bridges, following the contours of the land, listening for the gulp of guppies. There was so much space for imagination and storytelling, but I wished to be somewhere more exciting than the white skies of suburban Detroit. Back then, I did not consider my hometown to be a beautiful place. Two-story brick houses with green lawns and major thoroughfares named for the number of miles out from the city line. Everything was too neat and tidy, familiar, easy. I wanted a faster pace, a place where I didn't know every detail of the landscape.

1993-1994, New York City

Three weeks after college graduation, I moved to New York City to work without pay as an intern at a trade newspaper. I hoped to turn it into a full-time, paid position, but until it was, I slept in the extra bedroom of a cousin's Upper East Side apartment.

City living wasn't as easy as I had expected. My first time at the grocery, I left behind a bag of paid-for items. Until then, I'd pushed a cart to my car and loaded bags of groceries in the trunk. But in the city, I'd have to carry everything in my hands. In my cousin's apartment, I realized I didn't have everything I'd purchased. My stomach clenched. I bolted out of the apartment and ran down the street, tears streaking my cheeks, feeling like a Midwestern fool.

The bag was waiting for me at the checkout line beside a kind-smiling cashier. She said something like, "It's okay, love," and handed me the bag. That's when I started to consider how much the people make a place. Before that moment, I'd felt very alone in the big city. All it took was a stranger's kindness and my cousin's open door to help me settle in, to feel like I could belong there. Then, I could notice the sound of footsteps on sidewalks and the misty scent of rain cooling the pavement.

That summer, I rollerbladed in Central Park, falling on the grass with a full heart and no fear. I went on dates in Chinatown, joined a writers' workshop in Greenwich Village, rode the subway to poetry readings, ate half-priced sushi during happy hour with my coworkers. The screaming trains and honking taxis and brisk click of fast-walking feet became familiar, even soothing. I stopped being scared of what I didn't know.

I lived in New York for one full year. That winter, six snowstorms swept through the city, stranding parked cars under heaps of snow as trucks cleared the streets. Subway platforms were packed with people waiting for the few trains that could get through.

I shared a one-bedroom apartment with a childhood friend named Lydia. We had a small bathroom with no window and a galley kitchen. Everything was beige—the cabinets, the walls, the toilet. We divided the living room in two to create a smaller bedroom, where I slept. Out my window, tall buildings speared the sky, and the *rat-a-tat-tat* of road construction lulled me to sleep. I built an Ikea desk badly, a leg bent around a cracked bolt, the whole thing slanting as I sat there to write, to fill out grad school applications, to write letters home. After work, Lydia and I stripped down to shorts and bras, sipped white wine, played jazz on the radio and cooked chicken for dinner.

I left before I could let the fast pace of a never-sleeping city seep inside me. A spot opened in my newspaper's Capitol Hill bureau, and I took it. New York had been fun, but it never felt like home. I wanted a place that was mine, to belong where I landed.

1994-1996, Washington, D.C.

Done with busy-city living, I moved to a post-war walkup in Bethesda, Maryland that backed up to the National Institutes of Health. I lived with my friend Celine, blocks from restaurants and shops and old homes with manicured lawns. Eventually, I got a new job as a reporter at the local Jewish newspaper. On weekends, I rode a mountain bike along dirt trails in Rock Creek Park or wrote poems at a friend's farm in the foothills of the Shenandoah mountains.

Once I left the clogged highways of the capitol, I turned the music loud and drove fast. Once, I wrote a poem about yearning to move to the mountains, with a line that said, "If I could rent a U-Haul, I'd move my life here."

"You *can* rent a U-Haul—for like twenty bucks," my grad school professor said. "What's that about?"

I was always yearning for a different me in a future life. Dreams of new places called to me, but never the reality of the place where I was. I thought I'd find myself somewhere new, be happier, less lonely, more fulfilled and know that it was home. But new places scared me—it was too much effort to meet people and learn the streets, to start completely over and fresh with no one to guide my way. The not knowing made me lonely. If I didn't have a job or a partner or friends or family, how would I fit in?

Would anyone see me, turn at the sound of my voice? I'd always considered myself strong, independent, rebellious, but deep down, I feared I wouldn't fit anywhere—a Jew in a Christian world, a lover of nature afraid to sleep under the stars for all the strange sounds that come in the dark.

Suburban Detroit, 1996-ongoing

After three years in Washington, D.C., I returned to Detroit, longing for the familiarity of family and the friendly Midwest. I've been here ever since, and now, it's my children who believe they'll find their true home, their best self, somewhere else.

"Why do we live in Michigan when there are such beautiful places in the world?" asks my daughter, Eliana.

We are driving along a winding road on the northwest coast of Maui, a bucket-list trip for my fiftieth birthday. The waves are calm to the west but fierce as we drive north, the ocean thundering against a rocky shoreline. The water swirls in a foam of white and turquoise and deep blue. No wave stays in any one place for long.

The ocean kicks up with the wind—or is it the wind that infuriates the waves? I forget where force begins and ends, where sky meets land, what leads the way. This is a beautiful place. But beauty doesn't guarantee happiness or a feeling of home.

I know that now, but my girl may not—impatient, beautiful, yearning to go and do and see. So much like me.

At eighteen, I wanted to see everything. By twenty-six, the place was less important than the people. When I returned home, Michigan was different to me. The trees soared and swayed, offering poetic shade on hot days. The Great Lakes held stories of sunken vessels in their cold waves, sailboats shifting atop diamond waters. The place I once found gray and empty came alive with meaning and possibility because I finally knew how to be happy anywhere.

I no longer wanted to conquer the world or believed it was even necessary—I only wanted to embrace it, to notice its precious details, to find happiness in the quiet moments. In Hawaii, the hibiscus flower blooms yellow in the morning and dies by nightfall, turning a vibrant red before falling slowly to the ground. The sameness of this routine happens day after day, and it is a beautiful plant, with a small journey, content in its destiny.

"I'd rather live in a place of great beauty than a flat state named for the bodies of water that surround it," my daughter insists.

"There is beauty everywhere," I say. "In Michigan, there are hills, trees and cold, clear waters from glacial lakes. There are gray days everywhere." But she's not ready to hear this.

I once believed I would find a place where I would feel most at home. Where I could be my best self. Where the roads and contours of the land would rise up to greet me as a daughter of the terrain. It took a decade for me to learn that the place doesn't make the person. To learn how to feel at home in my skin.

We park the car and climb over rocks to peer at a blow hole. The ocean reaches its angry fingers in to spray water up and out. Signs everywhere warn of the dangers of getting too close. Every year, visitors are sucked in, caught in the anger of the tides. And yet, people cascade down the mountain, clamber over slick rocks to witness the beauty up close.

A rainbow arches over the landscape. In Judaism, a rainbow is God's promise that he will never destroy the world, no matter how terrible the people are. In Hawaii, there are rainbows nearly every day.

Beauty is defined as the quality in a person or thing that gives pleasure to the senses, exalts the mind or spirit. John Keats said a thing of beauty is a joy forever.

I come from a wandering people perpetually in search of freedom. Generations have instilled in me the message that home resides within, and finally I know that wherever I go, I am home.

Coming Back to the Fruit

9

— · —

MAKING GRANDMA'S CHICKEN SOUP

*B*uy a whole chicken. Cut it into eighths. Rinse and pat dry. Place the pieces in a deep pot and fill with water. Add a tablespoon of salt, a teaspoon of pepper. Bring it to a boil then skim off the fat.

I stare at the recipe on lined notebook paper, some of the blue ink smudged by drops of water, the edges stiff and yellowed by all the time that has passed since I first wrote the words. I was 23 and living near Washington, D.C., and I couldn't return to my family's home near Detroit for Passover that year. Instead, Grandma Sheila taught me over the phone how to make her soup.

Today, I no longer need to look at the recipe to make it, but I do anyway. When I see my writing on the page, I can still hear her voice, though she has been gone for eight years. "Buy fresh dill," she would say. "Fresh dill makes all the difference."

Flat parsley and, if you can find it, parsley root. A thick parsnip cut into chunks. A whole onion, quartered and floating. A handful of celery stalks, cut into fourths.

My kids have always loved carrots, so I include more of it than any other vegetable. I don't add ingredients in steps, like Grandma did. I throw everything in as quickly as I can clean and chop.

The first time I made Grandma's soup, I sat at the table in my quiet apartment in Bethesda, Maryland, lifted a spoonful to my mouth and closed my eyes. With the flavor of fresh dill on my tongue, I was home, sitting around the holiday table with everyone I loved, my grandfather's jowls bouncing as he laughed, my grandmother smiling at his side, surveying all she'd created.

It's not hard to make a pot of soup. It just takes time. I can also make quiche, bake muffins, roast meat in onion, garlic, ginger, ketchup and brown sugar. And then, when I sit with people I love and they exclaim or sigh over the food I made, I feel like I have created a whole world in one meal.

I started cooking when I was a newly minted college graduate living in New York City. After taking two subway trains to my midtown office, working a full day and trekking home, cooking was one way to unwind with my roommate in the tiny apartment we shared. We'd strip down to bras and shorts, sip white wine, listen to jazz on the radio and pound chicken breasts. We'd boil water for pasta, peel and chop cucumbers, slice tomatoes, dice scallions, tear lettuce for salad. When we sat down to eat after all that effort, all the patient waiting for the food to be ready, whatever we made tasted like manna from heaven, as if the salt from our sweat had seasoned it.

Years later, when my children were babies, I never bought a jar of food. I mashed banana or avocado, made soup with sweet potato and zucchini. I shredded chicken onto their highchair trays, crumbled matzah balls for them to fist into their mouths. I loved the act of creating something nourishing from simple ingredients.

Since my grandmother was a skilled cook and baker, and my mother, just one generation later, didn't enjoy making food from scratch, I assumed that most American women had moved away from home cooking during the first wave of feminism. However, the shift had started earlier, in the 1940s, when Campbell's produced ready-to-eat meals to lighten the burden on housewives. This was a full twenty years before Betty Friedan published *The Feminine Mystique*, and, as Michael Pollan wrote in 2009 in *The New York Times*, "taught millions of American women to regard housework, cooking included, as drudgery, indeed as a form of oppression."

I don't think Grandma felt oppressed in the kitchen.

She didn't cook solely to keep us alive, but to keep us loved. She had an ease about her when she prepared food, even when she made gefilte fish from scratch, which takes all day and smells up the house. It didn't seem hard for her to create beautiful dishes; it seemed to relax, perhaps even invigorate, her.

Grandma taught me not to rush anything—whether recipes or the routine of daily life. It has taken me years to embrace her message. While I wait for salmon to cook, I can fit in three other activities or pause in the silence. I've learned to pour a glass of wine, put music on and feel the beat while my creations simmer.

In Grandma's kitchen, a little radio hung from the underside of a cabinet. She'd tune it to a classical station and hum along. Every morning, she'd spend an hour applying her makeup and arranging her hair that was washed weekly at a salon. She'd choose an outfit, secure the necklace with child-shaped pendants enumerating her great-grandchildren (eighteen by the end of her life), enjoy a cup of coffee and a bite of breakfast.

Once I returned to the Detroit suburbs to raise my own family, Grandma would drive to my house with treats for my four children—small plastic bags each containing exactly the same number of M&M's plus a Dum-Dum lollipop and a tiny box of raisins. She and I watched my kids build forts from blankets and pillows, jump in puddles, pump their legs on swings. We talked about my work, my parenting, my marriage, and I'd ask about her life—anything just to hear the cadence of her voice and the wisdom in her words.

In forty-two years, though, we never cooked together. Grandma prepared feasts for me, and later I made meals for her. Indeed, after Grandpa died, she came to my house for Shabbat meals that featured her recipes as well as some of my own.

I have inherited many of her cookbooks—*The Settlement Cook Book* by Lizzie Black Kander, *A Treasure for My Daughter* from a Hadassah chapter in Montreal and *The Jewish Cook Book* by Mildred Grosberg Bellin—with her cursive scrawled in the margins or on slips of paper.

"Enjoy the process of making something," I imagine Grandma saying to me. "Let it take the time it needs. Watch how the flavors come together and relish the magic of satisfying those you feed."

I learned recently that the word "restaurant" comes from the French verb *restaurer*, to revive or restore. First used in the 16th century, "restaurant" referred to a soup sold by street vendors as a cure for exhaustion—a remedy so sustaining that it changed the language.

On the same weathered paper as Grandma's soup recipe

are her instructions for making matzah balls. Sometimes I get them perfect—fluffy and light. When I rush the process, they end up hard and heavy, a struggle to cut with a spoon. When I make them right, Grandma whispers her approval in my ear, watching over my shoulder as I dip my hands in cold water before forming each ball. She's reminding me to slow down, that good food takes time.

This essay was first published in HADASSAH MAGAZINE on March 28, 2022, https://www.hadassahmagazine.org/2022/03/28/at-passover-remembering-my-grandma-and-her-chicken-soup/

10

OYSTERS

The oysters arrived on a paper plate, craggy half-shells pooling ocean brine. A server slung a basket of napkins, vinegar and cocktail sauce on the table. Dan lifted a shell and slurped. I forked one and bit into the softness, closing my eyes. I breathed in through my nose to taste more fully. These were bigger than any oysters I'd ever seen—palm-length, light gray. I texted a picture of them to my father: "I'm back!"

I was emerging from a decade of living as an Orthodox Jew, shedding the cloak of off-limits shellfish and figuring out my own way to sanctify food. I preferred to follow flavor, experience and exploration, not rules dictated by ancient rabbis and preserved by homogeneous communities. I'd grown up in a secular Jewish home where my father saw expensive and exotic meals as his reward for hard work, his antidote to a bland childhood. Food became the way we connected.

Although it was my choice to embrace Orthodox Judaism, I'd missed sampling elegant dishes and creative concoctions. Instead of traveling to new destinations and tasting culture through cafes, airport kiosks and roadside eateries, I'd had to plan vacations around kosher hotspots and canned goods with rabbi-approved *hekshers* (symbols indicating kosher supervision). I'd missed learning a place through its menus. Most of all, I'd missed savoring flavors with my father.

***

Dad first flew on a plane at eighteen. Much later, when he made his way as a scrap metal entrepreneur and could afford fancy vacations, he took full advantage, wanting to visit corners of the world that as a boy, he hadn't known existed. My family went on cruises and to Caribbean resorts when blue-cold Michigan winters grew bitter. Japan was Dad's favorite destination, where he ate *shabu shabu*, named for the sound of the ingredients—thin strips of meat and vegetables—cooking in hot water tableside. Dad ventured to China when few Americans were brave enough to go, and he insisted that Chinese food as we knew it was nothing like the real thing.

My father regaled us with stories about what an awful cook his mother was. All I remember of Grandma Sarah's kitchen were the Keebler cookies she kept hidden on a high shelf to reward our good behavior and the soft tuna fish sandwiches she made when Dad and I visited on Sundays. He insisted her culinary ineptitude was legendary: She burned toast, cooked meat until it was tough as shoe leather, had no sense for a delicate sauce or a velvety marinade. "Where do you think I learned to eat eggs with ketchup?" he'd say.

Shrimp was a regular feature on our family table—cold with cocktail sauce or sauteed with rice pilaf. Once, my father returned from a business trip to Boston with a crate of live lobsters that my mother boiled for dinner. I consumed clams like popcorn, dragged through melted butter. And grilled swordfish was a weekday favorite as familiar in the rotation as breaded chicken—beside a starch and vegetable.

But oysters were our thing. I first tried Oysters Rockefeller in a white-cloth restaurant. Smothered in spinach, butter and cheese, their slimy texture was indiscernible, so I had no childish objections. It wasn't long before raw oysters beckoned, first swiped through cocktail sauce and soon in nothing but their brine with lemon squeezed over top. I loved the taste and the texture—smooth, fresh, comfortingly salty. When I ate oysters, I felt a surge of energy as if I became part of the ocean itself, womb-like waves swirling around me.

***

The place where Dan and I were eating oysters was less a restaurant than a small building on a wooden dock planted on poles in the Pacific Ocean. We'd almost missed the turn as Dan drove along a two-lane rural road in Oregon, and I navigated from a piece of paper he'd printed before the trip. A folder of loose papers scattered along the back seat of the rental car. We were eight months into a passionate relationship, on the heels of disappointing first marriages. I was learning that he was great at vacation research, scouring the internet for restaurants and hiking trails that most people missed.

I saw the similarities between Dan and my father. They both liked to sum things up. Dad was fond of sayings like "People who want to get married get married," and "It's better than the alternative." Dan smiled a lot and says, "It's all good, baby!" After work, Dan mowed the lawn or sat on the couch with me watching TV, while Dad read 1,000-page crime novels or the *New York Times*. They were both voracious readers, and they made friends easily—on a plane, in line at a store. At conferences, people swarmed to talk to them.

Both my husband and my father dealt in scraps. My husband an archivist, my dad a scrap metal entrepreneur, they devoted their lives to turning other people's trash into useful things. Dan saved stories, photos and documents, while Dad melted and crushed the wheels from old office chairs or discarded metal shavings into the bones of buildings, the foundation of new creations.

They could unclog any drain, repair any leaky downspout, replace any faucet, attach any light fixture. Dad insisted I keep operating manuals for every piece of equipment I bought, though he was the only one who ever read them. Dan took care of all my IT needs—transferring data when I upgraded my iPhone or computer, troubleshooting when my email wouldn't sync, and setting up new devices when I didn't have the patience for it (which was always).

Most importantly, both men accepted me for who I am—Dan completely, Dad about ninety percent. For example, when I wanted to go to graduate school for creative writing, my father offered to pay for law school. "Lighten up, Lynnie," he would say whenever I came to him with hurt feelings. But his ninety percent acceptance was the most acceptance I found in my family of origin. Feeling like I didn't belong among the people who'd raised me propelled me toward Orthodox Judaism: I craved complete acceptance.

I thought following rules would make me acceptable to others. The real me was too intense, outspoken and brazen: I call it like it is. I'm honest and direct. And that made me "too much" for certain friends, family members and most boyfriends, who ultimately discarded me. So I gave myself up.

As a religious woman, I played a part—wearing the long-skirt, long-sleeved uniform; tucking my curly hair into hats; and not speaking in front of men. I sat in the synagogue's women's section behind a barrier to witness the service men loudly led. At first, following rules felt easy, a relief from the secular life I'd known, where following my instincts had led to so much rejection and hurt.

When I became religious, I didn't mind walking two miles to synagogue on the Sabbath instead of driving, and it was nice to have one day every week without the phone ringing or the TV blaring. What made me sad was that I could no longer eat with my father.

Though he was proud of his Jewish identity, Dad grew up on the streets of Detroit, where he was teased and punched for being a Jew. He never stepped foot in a synagogue from the day of his Bar Mitzvah until he married my mother at thirty. Then he went only reluctantly, on the High Holidays, and napped in his seat for most of the service.

Before I chose the Orthodox world, I turned to him for advice and guidance, and our best conversations took place over juicy cheeseburgers and pop-in-your-mouth shrimp cocktail. Dad hated that I embraced religion. We no longer had a table to connect over; my table had so many rules, such boring food, and his seemed very far away.

***

It didn't take me long to learn that hypocrisy is not the sole domain of the secular. Much of my insecurity in childhood stemmed from the gossip and judgment in my affluent enclave: You couldn't belong if you didn't wear tight black clothing, blow your curls out smooth, and eventually attend University of Michigan or Michigan State University before moving back to the Detroit suburbs, marrying a Jewish guy, and having two or three babies.

I saw the Orthodox world through rosy lenses. Since one of the rabbis who welcomed me in displayed a sign on his dining room table that said, "Thank you for not speaking *lashon hora* (gossip)," I believed everyone strove to watch their words. Since modesty was mandated, I figured women would wear subdued colors and A-lines and focus on spirituality, not appearances. But the wealthiest religious women wore skintight, curve-hugging clothes that barely fell below the knee upon sitting, and I experienced more gossip, judgment and dismissal than ever. When I started wearing pants again and uncovered my hair, two close friends dropped me like a hot potato.

Where rules are rigid, people bend in extreme ways. In the Orthodox world, the acting out was legendary: pious men seeking prostitutes, closet KFC eaters, wig-wearing women who run basement businesses and never pay taxes. The enclave I had been so thrilled to discover turned out to be a world of secrets.

Unhappily married, disillusioned by religion, and yearning for love, I divorced and left Orthodoxy at thirty-seven, reclaiming the freedom to bare my arms, drive on Saturdays, and spontaneously drop into a new restaurant without consulting supervising rabbis. Soon after, I met Dan on a Jewish dating site.

When I became Orthodox, I wanted to make life simpler, but it never really is. I wanted to know my role and be rewarded for filling it. For instance, I thought if I were the doting, obedient wife, I'd be happy. But I realized that I far preferred having choices. Having choices meant deciding who to love and how to love them. Though my childhood was imperfect, my father taught me to appreciate moments, celebrate good times, experience the world, and eat new foods without fear. If that made me too intense for some people, it would make me exhilarating to others.

I'd missed years of birthday dinners at iconic Detroit restaurants, twenty relatives chattering and passing plates. I'd endured pre-packaged kosher food at cousins' weddings, feeling so on the outskirts of my family of origin that those happy days made me sad. Now, on Friday nights when my children go to their father for Shabbat, Dan cooks for me—white beans with garlic and greens, mussels in wine with crusty bread, a charcuterie of tangy meats, creamy cheeses, and crisp apple slices.

One of the best outcomes of rejecting a religious lifestyle was reconnecting with my father through weekly lunch dates. For years, we chose different restaurants each week—Beverly Hills Grill for burgers or huevos rancheros, Leeza's for omelets and toast with greasy hash browns, Steve's Deli for matzah ball soup and Maurice salads. No matter how busy work was, I looked forward to those islands of time during an ordinary day—just Dad and me savoring bites of stacked sandwiches, scrambled eggs, lentil soup or dripping burgers still pink in the middle, and lingering in conversation.

***

My father died early in 2020 after two years of battling an aggressive blood cancer. For most of his illness, Dad kept his calm strength, pretty chill about a terminal diagnosis. He never lingered in bad news, knowing he could do nothing to change it. The illness made him crave red meat, so in his final months, whenever he grew tired of hospital food, I got us corned beef sandwiches from Al's, his favorite hole-in-the-wall deli on Woodward Avenue. The sandwiches were still warm when I returned to his room. We sat close, leaning over the tray beside his bed, biting into the soft bread, the hot meat, the tangy mustard, grease dripping down our fingers.

Three days before he died, Dad ended up in the emergency room, disoriented and badly in need of blood. He swam in and out of lucidity, mumbling about chess. My mother dismissed his words as incoherence, but I knew the dying say things we need to hear, so I leaned in. "I need to make the right move," he said.

"I know, Dad," I replied. "You will."

We sat around him, nervous energy pulsing. It was a small room, bare white walls and no windows. Outside, winter raged in sleeting rain and blowing snow. Suddenly, I needed a corned beef sandwich.

Someone ran out in the cold and drove to Al's. When the sandwiches arrived, I peeled back the paper wrappings, covered my lap in napkins to catch the grease. I sank my teeth in and closed my eyes. The scent, the taste, the texture, the memory transported me to a place where my father was smiling and we were talking easy and long.

Dad opened his eyes. "What's that smell?" he said. "Get that out of here."

I wrapped up the sandwich, stuffed it in a paper bag, and took it to the waiting room. I no longer had an appetite anyway.

A month later, I took my family to the Florida Keys, where we ate key lime pie, Dad's favorite. I relished the soft tangy filling, crumbling crust, light and airy cream on top. I ate seafood fresh from the ocean and bloody steaks in open-air restaurants. The oysters were smaller there but just as tangy and reassuring. I talked about him and cried a little with every bite.

***

The day Dan and I ate those amazing oysters began with a forest hike, another of Dan's internet finds. We switchbacked through tall trees downhill to a deserted ocean beach. When we reached the rolling, thunderous waves, we felt like the only people in the world. We took off our shoes to let the water wash over our aching feet. We sat on the sand and listened to the surf. Then we wound our way back up through the trees to our car and drove past windblown vineyards and the Tillamook cheese factory to a little building without a sign perched on a dock over the sea. An arching crane dumped oysters from the ocean onto the dock, salt water dripping through the planks. Minutes later, those oysters landed on our plates.

The buzz of conversation in the eatery hummed. Dan smiled, brushed his fingers over my leg. Our knees touched under the table. Servers bustled around the small space, between tables and a counter of refrigerated cases offering just-caught clams, oysters and squid, fresh salads, home-made coleslaw. When the door opened, I heard the roar of the ocean.

My father responded to my message: "Yes!"

This essay first appeared in PORRIDGE MAGAZINE on September 25, 2021, https://porridgemagazine.com/20 21/09/25/oysters-lynne-golodner/

11

— · —

GOING TO INDIA

The Leaving

Between the tropical forest and the Dehradun airport, men watched planes land and leave. Arms overhanging the fence, chins on hands, they stared.

What did they see? People coming and going when they could not. Stories winging away in the vast sky. The remarkability of flight itself, heavy and hot but lifting as easily as a butterfly.

My bags were heavy with everything I carried home. I hadn't wanted to visit India, but when a client invited me to accompany her yoga tour, to write blogs and photograph the journey, I couldn't say no. A free trip to the other side of the world! A place I would never otherwise go, away from my young children, into the humid heat of the Himalayan foothills.

I didn't sleep for a month before the trip. A mystic therapist told me to close my eyes and identify the fear. *I was raised in comfort, taught to travel as a tourist, watch life from a distance. I don't know how to get close.*

It surprised me when, on the tarmac, I swallowed tears. I didn't want to leave. I did not yearn to return to my easy life. In India I had found a contentment, a calm, that eluded me at home.

Do we all dream of something different? Could the swift current of the Ganges and the abundant stars in the night sky be enough for me? Or was it only beautiful because I could leave it?

The Place

Sometimes a place changes you. A place you never dreamed of visiting, never even knew about, but when you go, the very feel of the earth beneath your feet tells a story you want to believe. Of course, it's easy (and dangerous) to fantasize that life is better, easier, more beautiful and fragrant, in a distant place.

Cliché—an overused phrase that lacks original thought, a stereotype.

A white woman boards a train in India, clutching her backpack and camera bag, squatting in the first-class bathroom to pee over the hole in the floor, urine streaming onto the tracks. Looks askance at the legless man pulling up the aisle before the train leaves the station, hand out, eyes begging her to see him, to drop money in his palm. She stares at the back of the seat in front of her. Like she'd been taught all her life, as her parents whisked her away on colonial vacations to hole up in all-inclusive resorts with tall walls to keep out the natives. As her parents' car whizzed past a man on the side of a freezing highway in her hometown, his sign claiming he had a family to feed and would take anything she could give. And even as she thinks *hometown*, she knows that isn't entirely true, because she lived on the outskirts of the dangerous city, in the safe and sleepy suburbs, and when the locked car ventured south of 8 Mile, she knew to *look everywhere else:* the gleaming skyline by a fast-moving river, the radio dial, the interior temperature of the brand-new car, so she could ignore how the man's knuckles blazed red from too long in the cold.

Had I learned nothing? I came seeking transformation but at a distance, perfectly fulfilling the elitist trope that I knew so well: willing and able to experience a tourist-safe version of India while heart-crying at the poverty around me. What did I do to change it other than sponsor the education, room and board of three orphans I hugged near

Lakshman Jula? I wanted to bring them all home, give
them a different life, but that was impossible. We can only
change our station slightly, if at all, and besides, who says
my way would be better for them?

I say I changed when I went to India, when I went
to Bali, when I went to Israel, when I kissed the pink
stones and believed they could absorb my prayers. The
change is in the going, in walking down unfamiliar streets.
I am privileged enough to go, and when I carry revelations
home in my bursting suitcases, I don't think about how
my whiteness allowed this transformation. I don't think
about how I expect everyone to speak to me in English,
to understand my every word. I don't think about how
careful I was to not swallow shower water in fear of ending
up sick, my delicate stomach unable to process foreign
microbes. I don't think about how I can't live as easily in a
new place as I might imagine.

The writer Jamaica Kincaid says in *A Small
Place,* "Every native of every place is a potential tourist,
and every tourist is a native of somewhere. Every native everywhere lives a life of overwhelming and crush-
ing banality and boredom and desperation and depression...every native would like to find a way out."

I believe I have seen the world, but I have only seen a tiny
corner of it, a whitewashed, neat and clean, tidy corner of

a world I can never inhabit because I must return home to sleep safe behind locked doors and under old quilts. It doesn't take long to absorb back into the fluffy comfort of my privilege. In fact, that is something I never leave, clinging to it in the darkness, dialing its number as my emergency contact.

If you can't afford to go anywhere distant and different, does that mean you can't open your mind and let new ideas drip in? When I travel, I gain perspective, realize what matters (being good, doing good, loving my fellow humans) and what doesn't (racing to acquire more things, earning evermore money, filling my calendar until I pray for someone to cancel on me).

I became a cliché in India. Finding meaning in the old stones of an empty ashram, Beatles lyrics for graffiti on the walls of crumbling buildings. The words of white men spray-painted across a place no longer inhabited. I was the blackbird, capturing pictures of leaves and stones arranged to say *all you need is love*. In my hired cars and clean hotels, eating food approved for western stomachs (that was the phrase they used, I swear), carrying a Z-pack in case I accidentally sipped local water, choking down antibiotics to thwart fever, chase away chills. Back home, I never listened to the Beatles. What made me find salvation in their words in the tangled hills of northern India?

The Difference

In India, whole families balance on motor bikes, toss paper plates onto the street when they finish eating. Beside street vendors selling sweets, people kneel in prayer. Rivers promise redemption: the faithful wade in fully clothed, pulling the water over themselves, hoping for rebirth.

In my home, prayers are private, immersions quiet. We designate days for worship and spend the rest running. We think our way is better, that we understand what makes a good life.

I never wanted to visit India. It was far from home and clogged with people, and I was afraid of the stories in my head, of garbage and beggars, oblivious to the same in my hometown.

But going changed me. I became humble, reflective. I poured warm oil on my hair to soften it, used less toilet paper because there was less to use. I became okay with everything: rising at four a.m., wearing the same clothes again and again, eating soupy lentils in a squat at the Golden Temple, peeing over a hole in a first-class train speeding toward the highest mountains, walking rain-wet streets in a quiet dawn without word or thought. I cloaked myself in the quiet and saw that a good life does not need clutter obscuring the view of loping hills. That stripping away everything might actually be the first step to understanding.

The Fantasy

Because I was her guest, I followed the yoga instructor's every step. I'll call her J. She insisted I share her hotel room, trail after her before the dawn and invert my body into downward dog for eleven minutes, until I grew nauseous. She called the shots; I merely recorded them.

"Maybe I'll find a husband here," J giggled, her blonde hair and golden skin drawing the gaze of dark men who didn't speak her language. "Aren't the turbans sexy?" She smiled as they whistled. Was it a fetish? Objectification? Both sides dehumanizing, but ours was worse somehow.

I had love in my life—a new husband and four young children. In our shared room, she played mantra music on repeat to help her sleep.

"Will I ever find a love like you have?" she asked.

"I'm sure you will," I replied. My father always said that people who want to get married get married. I told her what she wanted to hear.

I didn't say that I didn't quite believe my father. Not everyone finds a great love. Some people just make do with what they have. And, as the leader of her American yoga community, she was adored, never known. Infatuation doesn't make for lasting bedfellows.

I wanted to tell her that pretending to be someone she's not only confuses the search. For self and for place. For a true definition of home.

I'd heard her backstory: raised Christian, WASP-y, one failed marriage, three grown sons, long blonde hair in waves down her back, a pierced nose, a flat belly. She walked naked from the bed to the shower as if I wouldn't care. I had no choice; I was there on her dime.

What was she doing in white parachute pants and mala beads around her neck? Someone else's prayer necklace as her jewelry. Appropriating another's sacred tradition, bastardizing it like tourists do. Claiming it as her new spiritual path. But that was a story I wouldn't write, the yoga instructor in all-white, hair twisted into a turban. A trip of pretending, like all good voyages.

I sound bitter, maybe even unappreciative. Perhaps because J reminded me too closely of my privileged upbringing, where I was taught to keep my distance. I am grateful to her for taking me to a place I never wanted to visit, for forcing me to face my fear of losing control, encouraging me to learn a language I didn't yet understand. In India, I bathed in milky humility and came home quieter.

The Art of Believing

At the Golden Temple, I walked barefoot on cold marble. I had no choice. They demand your shoes before you can go in. In my American mind, I wondered if I'd get my shoes back at the end. In the Amrit Sarovar, the pool of nectar, fat orange koi waggled in the depths. Sikhs welcome anyone who believes in God; 100,000 people visit daily.

I'm not sure I believe, but no one asked. What is it to believe? And what is God? Would they really turn me away if I said I was uncertain? But, come on, people! No one can know a God in the sky, a deity we can't see, waving magic hands over all the tiny people like marionettes on strings lifted and dropped down to the ruddy surface of an uneven planet. This talk of God exhausts me. No one can really know, so why make it a criterion for entry? Even the gatekeepers can't be sure. Doubt lurks in the dark corners of every mind. To doubt is human, to believe is desperate. And anyway, we all say what we imagine others need to hear.

I have spent a lifetime searching for meaning in the mundane. I may have found it in the simple task of watching the ghee pot, kneading the dough for naan, a barefoot man squatting over a hot fire. Don't his thighs burn? His knees shake?

Or perhaps in the rhythmic chanting of the Guru. The throbbing mass snaking its way inside to listen and watch, scarves wrapped around our heads. There are universal truths connecting us all, and modesty is one of them. For a decade, I'd lived as an Orthodox Jew with my first husband, covering my hair to fit into his world. When I left him, I donated all my elegant and expensive hats, freeing my curls in the bright sun.

But in India, I didn't resent the mandate to cover up. It was temporary, for one. I could don a costume, play a part. In Amritsar, I didn't mind wrapping my head. I can wear another person's modesty just fine and without complaint. It meant nothing to me, so I bundled up and inched along in a caterpillar of people past chanting men, the rhythm constant, the words a vibration. I could be obedient for a time. Holiness a harmony pulsing.

The Point of It All

After the divorce, I took my children to different synagogues, seeking wisdom and a place to belong. When I married Dan, we recited Jewish, Native American and ancient Hindu blessings under my grandfather's prayer shawl, on the hottest day of summer. After, our children jumped in the lake fully clothed, like the pilgrims by the Ganges.

We joined a sprawling synagogue, but whenever we attended, someone asked, "Are you new?" After four years of not being known, we left in search of a place where we would be remembered.

I brought many things home from India. Wool blankets. Delicate scarves and sheer, embroidered shirts. Two heavy statues shipped ahead: one of Ganesh, remover of obstacles, and a Shiva Nataraja, lord of the dance. They arrived a month after I did, Shiva broken, the deity severed from its base of flames. I set the base in the garden where vegetation overtook it, weeds and grass snaking through and around the licking flames. I mounted Lord Shiva on the garage; he welcomes me home, reminds me that it is possible to break free. Ganesh sits on the piano, visible from my writing desk.

"You don't pray to those statues, do you?" asked my ex-husband.

Why did he care? Why did he think he had the right to ask? And why, even, did I answer?

"It's not my religion," I said. "But I see spirituality everywhere."

After that, he refused to enter my house, waiting for the children outside in the driving rain.

There was so much I didn't say to him, and I'm not sure he would have heard my words anyway. Like, *all people live in similar ways, even if we call our gods by different names*. I have the privilege of believing what I want, of picking and choosing. When I was married to him, I recited prayers, swaying like Orthodox Jews are supposed to, begging a God I didn't believe in to release me from doubt. I thought if I moved my lips and whispered the words, answers would come. But there was no bellowing voice, no lightning strike.

These days, my prayers are trees blowing in the wind, rivers and birds, deer prints in the snow.

The Transformation

I left Amritsar by train in the purple-dark, city lights infiltrating the dawn. Breakfast was milky chai, chopped fruit and thin pancakes doused in honey and coconut. We pulled suitcases past sleeping bodies on the cold concrete, on benches, under shuttered awnings, in the shadows of locked doors. Sleeping bodies everywhere, exposed to the elements. I wrapped my expensive shawl around me.

In first class, a bullet hole in the window spidered into a spiral of cracked glass. Eight hours to Haridwar, and then a car bumped us along winding mountain roads to

Rishikesh. Rain poured down, and our driver wiped fog from the windshield with a rag.

At the hotel, the proprietor draped marigold garlands around our necks. *You are on a journey of spiritual evolution,* he said. *You are seekers. This will be a transformation* .The next day would bring bright sun and monkeys in the trees.

For the right price, you can hire a private guide to take you through the abandoned ashram where the Beatles communed with the Maharishi. The rain-scented streets became familiar. The moving waters of the Ganges like kisses against the banks. I wore baggy pants and fitted shirts, wrapped my hair in a scarf and danced like I had nowhere else to be. At sunset, silent monks in orange robes led firelight ceremonies.

Every day, I recorded words and phrases and ideas, the details of wildflowers and damp alleys, glass-fronted shops and winding avenues. After two weeks, I boarded a plane for home. During a layover in Delhi, I ate in a restaurant overlooking the tarmac. There was news of a plane lost over the South China Sea. The world bustled like I remembered. Life became immediate again. I spread butter on a roll and wrote in a journal as planes lifted into the sky.

This essay first appeared in ADELAIDE LITERARY MAGAZINE on December 3, 2022: http://adelaidemaga

zine.org/2022/12/07/going-to-india-by-lynne-golodner/

12

— · —

A WALK IN BUDAPEST

First stop: *Medieval Jewish Prayer House – Középkori Zsidó Imaház*

American historians say Hungary's political system is dangerous, but conservatives find inspiration in its Christian government. I expected dark shadows in Budapest storefronts, people yearning for freedom. Instead, I found old stones with Hebrew etchings of familiar names, Jewish memory on the hilly side of a fast river.

The 14th century sanctuary is small, wooden chairs like sentries, Jewish stars a lattice, like clasped hands linking generations. On a modern Shabbat, old men pray time-worn words.

Ceilings rounded like Jerusalem architecture, just a four-hour flight from Holy Land. I came to Budapest to visit my son. Is it brave to return to the Eastern European

killing fields my ancestors fled? My 21st century son looks
for beauty in its stone streets, but my soul remembers.

Hebrew letters inked onto the plaster in this medieval
synagogue: a priestly blessing in David's shield, Hannah's
prayer arched with an arrow. *The bows of the mighty are
broken; those who stumble are girded with strength.* Red sec-
co ceiling painting discovered during a 1964 restoration.
Ancient words evoking an Ottoman siege of the nearby
Buda castle. Jews defending our neighbors, desperate to
blend.

Everywhere, the color red: in a velvet mantle over the
prayer podium, in a drape hiding ancient scrolls. The color
of blood, sacrifice, danger, courage. Also, the color of passion and anger.

This synagogue sits on a residential street behind a typical door, blending into a stucco landscape of sunrise yellow, summer peach, ballet pink. Congregants gather in a
cobbled courtyard, too like the hidden coves in this city
where Jews were shot. But here, no plaque commemorates
the dead, only tilting tombstones bearing familiar names.
No stories, only evidence that they lived. It's a working
synagogue come Friday dusk and Saturday dawn, a museum all the other days, paying homage to dead Jews.

We started here on our tour of Jewish Budapest, fore-
shadowing the story of my people in Hungary: we would

visit an equal number of exquisite sanctuaries and cold memorials. To be a Jew is a pendulum-swing existence, a constant living in extremes, a balance of horror and beauty. In this city, I ate matzah ball soup and goose-stuffed cabbage in fashionable restaurants with names like Mazel Tov and Rosenstein. I clapped at a klezmer concert on a Friday-night stage in the most cosmopolitan district. As if we had made it into popular culture.

One day, an old lady on a tram said she preferred Hungary to the United States. Hungarians believe in God, she said, and Americans love money. She studied economics in Washington, D.C., when she was young. Now 85, she's at home in her authoritarian country. This place brings her comfort, but I couldn't wait to leave. My son appreciated the public transportation and how cheap everything was. A country in flux: absolute adherence to rules and short supply on everything.

I came to Budapest on Election Day in a midterm year, wanting to avoid the results, for fear of extremists erasing democracy. But I couldn't escape. I landed in Europe to scrolling headlines: extremism defeated by candidates preaching justice for all. I settled into my seat and eased into a dreamless sleep.

Second stop: *Shoes on the Danube*

Thick boots, simple pumps and baby tie-ups bolted into concrete. A memorial of a moment, of Jews ordered by Nazis and eager Hungarians to step out of their valuable leather and wait for the bullets to kill them. Men, women, children, lovers, friends, families, shot, their limp bodies falling like dominoes into cold water, floating away in a red-stained river.

A bronze plaque, flush against the concrete, reads: *To the memory of the victims shot into the Danube by Arrow Cross Militiamen in 1944-45, erected 16th April 2005.*

They were Jews, dammit. I want to scream into the open sky. A cleansed message with no mention of the reason these precious people were murdered. Gunned down, one after another after another, falling limp against the cold and lonely earth.

This famous memorial sits in the shadow of the Hungarian Parliament, politicians just out of sight. You have to know the site is there to find it, descend wide steps toward milky-gray waters. No signs lead to horror.

In the rainy cold, squirming teenagers and barking teachers shuffle past the shoes. Are they oblivious because of their age or because they've consumed too much harsh memory? Do they even know the truth? Who does their teacher say died here, and why?

I wait for their noise to dissipate before kneeling, hot tears on wind-cold cheeks.

I would never vacation in an authoritarian country. But my son was studying math education in an old building with a Jewish star in its courtyard. So I slept in a nice hotel in the heart of a bustling city and tried to see past conflicting histories. Nothing screamed fascism. I never saw Viktor Orban and found the Communist ruin bar sort of hilarious. I could almost believe in safety.

Third stop: *Monument to the victims of the German occupation by Péter Párkányi Raab, Szabadság Square*

An eagle representing Nazi Germany beside archangel Gabriel, Hungary's patron. Isn't the eagle a symbol of American independence? And Gabriel a Jew? Of course, the eagle is a predator, soaring above all other life, eyeing prey with precision, swooping in unannounced.

The words, *remembering the victims* in Hungarian, English, German, Russian and Hebrew. The real memorial is just in front of this, wind-flapping pictures, handwritten notes, melted candles and old suitcases. And the concrete monument never mentions how eagerly Hungarians rounded up half a million Jewish neighbors for slaughter.

Ever had a dream you couldn't wake up from? You kick and flail in the muted night, claw toward the surface of awakening, but lay prone, heart thick with thumping. It's the Holocaust for me. I can never escape it, and I don't want to because it's become okay again to openly hate Jews. When I was young and single, I dreamt they were banging at my door in the dark night. I woke before they pushed inside but kept a hammer under my bed, just to be safe.

Photos dangle from barbed wire—a little girl in a tutu, a family of four headed to Auschwitz, the words: *anyone who denies the crimes of the past is ready to repeat them anytime.* An old, cracked suitcase, a mangled black shoe. A sweet picture of an older boy and his doting sister, cheek to cheek. Chiding comments by woke Hungarians, blaming their government for the slaughter of my people. A chilling photo of an old man with a cane, his shadow a family of four holding hands. An image of Volodymyr Zelensky, the Jewish president of Ukraine, fist raised, a slight smile on his young face, and the words: *He is standing up to a dictator. Because he knows what happens if you don't.*

I never used to vote in midterm elections. In the 1990s, it was just something we didn't do, complacent in budding careers and big-city living. Too busy loving the freedom of being American, believing we had it all.

When I turned religious and married a conservative man, I awakened. Our votes canceled each other out. I left him before another election came round, but in 2016, screens turned red with American fascism. *We might have to move to Canada,* I texted my thirteen-year-old daughter, who was at her father's house on Election Night. My ex emailed at one in the morning, *What the hell are you saying to the children?*

I'll do anything to protect my family. I'll do what it takes to keep us alive. This is Germany in the 1930s. They always come for us. Again and again and again.

Could I have prevented the fall of America in the 21st century by voting in the 20th? Did my adolescent indifference pave the way for fascism? How stupid I was to take freedom for granted, to give it all away.

Fourth Stop: *Klauzal Ter., "You shall tell your son..." Exodus 13:8*

The streets of Budapest are like spokes on a wheel. I was constantly confused by courtyards and alleys, old buildings with the memories of people running for their lives.

In the midst of twenty-one Michelin star restaurants, high fashion boutiques and gleaming hotels sits a quiet courtyard where people leave pebbles on a plaque.

"You shall tell your son..." Exodus 13:8

Another place Jews were rounded up and killed. Late fall, the leaves have fallen off two scraggly trees; the ground is cold. This is the third place today where Jews were murdered. I'm bored by repetition, like those teenagers on the banks of the Danube.

Tour groups crowd in to see where Jews were killed. An Italian explains the site. Then a Hebrew speaker. Above the memorial, red flowers on balconies are not yet winter-wilted. The patchy plasterwork of this building conflicts with a smooth new hotel next door. Horror and beauty are bedfellows.

Viktor Orban rode financial turmoil to power. Now, he's stacked the courts, claimed the media, created an "us or them" rhetoric—*real* Christian Hungarians versus immigrants and Muslims and gays. Jews are too small in number to matter. History saw to that.

What authoritarians do really well is make us afraid. But we are to blame for their rise. When they care more than we do, we get what we deserve.

There's a woman trying to reclaim Hungary: Katalin Cseh, a twentysomething leading the third biggest political party. We needn't choose between identities, she says. We can be everything all at once. If the 21st century is about identity, who do we want to be?

Fifth Stop: *Kazinczy Street Synagogue*

Built in 1913, with pale-blue walls, gold metallic stars of David and flower-shaped stained-glass windows. I've seen the Holocaust sites, and now I step inside a gorgeous synagogue. There's seating for women on the second floor, hard wooden benches for the men on the first, everyone facing the Ark and its holy scrolls. Only seventy parishioners regularly pray in this echoing sanctuary, in the same neighborhood where the young go at night, to ruin bars and raving restaurants.

A wedding song etched in metal: *kol sasson v'kol simcha,* the voice of joy and the voice of gladness. Jewish stars in glass and metal, wood and cloth. An art nouveau tapestry of identity. Sunlight filtering through skylights.

There is light everywhere, bright and shining. All the detail and thought that make a space holy. *Beautiful,* I say. *Yeah, but I came on Rosh Hashanah, and there were only a dozen old men,* my son says.

After college, I lived in Washington, D.C., the air thick

with humidity that peeled back the paper covers of my favorite books. It's not easy to live in a swamp, even if it's paved over with concrete and plaster.

Every city has a story, and versions vary between storytellers. In Budapest, a soaring synagogue tells me Judaism is accepted by all. But then I pass another plaque commemorating death. No memorial says the word *Jew*, not one expresses remorse or lament or even temporary sadness. It happened, so a story is told. We consume the words and keep walking.

Sixth stop: *Rumbach Street Synagogue*

Minaret towers and Moorish Alhambra columns, this place once drew Jews looking to reform old ways. Today, it's a concert venue and a museum.

A black stage fills the sanctuary. Circular windows with orange and turquoise flowers in the glass. A gold-etched, domed ceiling. Heavy lights hang low to illuminate the performance. A gaudy gold Ark. So many conflicting details. I don't know where to look first, or last.

Built in 1872, Jews worshipped here until it became a Holocaust deportation point. Then the Soviets came. Jews only returned to the crumbling façade in 2006, staking claim over decades of decay. Birds had flown in through holes in the roof, built nests in the sanctuary. Now, non-profits and charities inhabit upper-floor offices. An exhibit on the third floor details the history of Hungarian Jewry, through stories of the Pulitzer family. Jewish integration is everywhere. Come quick and take your seat. The show's about to begin.

Seventh stop: *Dohány Street Synagogue*

The largest European Jewish house of worship, the second largest synagogue in the world. Three floors for worshipers. Flags indicating the languages of visitors. It's so big and overwhelming that the rabbi must climb to a podium suspended above the first floor to be seen and heard.

I couldn't worship here. Too ornate, too big, too much of a show. Jews on display. I'd feel lonely. And I want to belong.

On the street, authoritarianism doesn't look different from democracy. The buildings are old and spackled, with exquisite frescos and metalwork. At a selfie store, employees wear pink, next to a Burger King, and buses and trams come frequently with an app that tells you in real time how long you'll wait. People hustle along. Little cars drive fast.

They won't stop for pedestrians, so look before you walk. Restaurants and cafes and bars, down narrow lanes, tuck into significant buildings, new life in old spaces. Across the river, as the craggy hills rise, people go to school and work and buy a kebab at a kiosk and pull coats tight as the winter wind sweeps down from tree-heavy hills. In subway stations, bakeries sell hot dough rolled in cinnamon and sugar and nuts. Sometimes, the sun shines, and the early mornings are cold, but people walk fast and smoke cigarettes in cafes with tiny cups of espresso.

Budapest looks like any place. Men wear the same tapered jeans as any European city, have the same haircuts. On the bus, all the shoes are black, and the people smile when you stand near them, gripping the pole for balance.

Final Stop: *Bethlen Gábortér 2, BSME Building*

The building where my son is studying used to house the National Institute for Jewish Deaf-Mute. Built in 1876, it expanded to include a synagogue in 1931. Before the Jews were rounded up, it was an elementary school and headquarters for various Jewish organizations.

In the courtyard is a memorial: a bronze tree between

narrowing walls of rocks contained by wire. The focal point: a concrete Star of David. All I can see is the wire keeping the rocks from tumbling down and burying everything.

There are no waves on the Danube. The water is milky gray and flat. Hungary is land-locked with only one river bending through the countryside. No easy way out.

I have circled the globe, adjusting to time zones and elevations. My son and I climbed to the highest point in Budapest. Midway, he scrambled up a sheer rock face. *Careful,* I called. *Don't lose your footing. Please stay safe.* At the top, the sun shone without interruption.

One night, my son played a piano in the rail station. The *click-click* of heels on marble beat a dull rhythm as his fingers flew over the ivory and a beautiful melody lifted to the high ceiling and out onto the tracks and through the open doors and over the wet pavement in the dark night. I was naïve to believe extremism lived abroad, to think hatred was an old story.

Authoritarianism is defined as *favoring complete obedience or subjection to authority as opposed to individual freedom; exercising almost complete control over the will of another.* I had no control over where my son studied, and I wanted him to know the world. *I've never been in a place where the Holocaust actually happened,* he said when he landed in Budapest. I spent a half century avoiding it.

But we go where we are called. After the hike, drenched in exertion, we ate hot dogs and hamburgers and salted fries in the café on the mountaintop. Then, we rode the chairlift down, tired from the enormity of it all.

This essay was first published in CONSEQUENCE FO-RUM on December 20, 2024. It first appeared at https://s ubstack.com/home/post/p-153367422and later here: https ://consequenceforum.org/a-walk-in-budapest/.

13

—·—

COMING BACK TO THE FRUIT

In June, I pick strawberries, crouching close to the ground, ankles burning as I pull soft berries from vines. The reddest ones stain my fingers. The sun is hot on the open field. In Michigan, the strawberries are ripe for just three weeks. My youngest son was born in the end of May, and I didn't want to miss the crop that year. He was small and new and slept against my body in a cloth sling, and sweat streamed down my cheeks as I squatted to pick the berries. It was hard—the kind of hard that you do because there is no other choice—and my older children, toddlers both, ran along the rows, palming berries and painting their faces as they ate them.

In July, it's blueberries. When my children were little, they ran up and down the rows, their little fat hands gripping the metal handles of plastic buckets. Eliana in golden wisps of pigtails, Asher with a head of curls, Shaya in my arms until he could scramble after them. The bushes were taller than all of us, the berries dusted gray in the slow of summer. We popped berries into our mouths like candy.

August and September, Michigan fields are full with apples. When I was a child, I climbed ladders to reach the highest branches. No one worried about liability then, and safety was relative. There's a picture of my sister, brother and me in the orchard, all smiling. Every year, I take my children to the apple orchards, the scent of fall on the wind and a late-autumn sun burning our skin. Even now, the kids are grown, but still they come with me because there is something freeing about being in the orchards. The lack of noise, perhaps, or the rush of wind, or the sweet-tart scent of too-ripe apples hitting the ground and fermenting in the late-day sun. When I think of the fall, I hear the buzz of bees and taste a fat drop of honey. Everything comes ripe in this part of the world then, the colors at their height before everything goes gray for the long and tedious winter.

In the aftermath of the Hamas massacre on October 7, 2023, Israeli fields laid fallow. Farmers were called up to serve in the rescue and retaliation just when strawberries were ripening, and day laborers weren't allowed in. Some of my friends flew there to help pick. Things that grow always need harvesting, even in a time of war. I wanted to go. Desperately. But something always got in the way.

I know the seasons of the year by the crops ready for

picking. And then, I feel close to the earth, nourished by the work of my hands. I was raised to believe that Jews were professionals—lawyers, doctors, accountants—not farmers, but the only Jewish nation, Israel, is an agricultural wonder. The Israeli agriculture market generates some $6.92 billion annually and is estimated to grow by nearly five percent each year. Israel exports an incredible amount of fresh produce and is a global leader in agricultural technology. With more than half of its acreage not suitable for farming and water in scarce supply, it's a wonder that Jewish pioneers could turn dry and dusty cracked earth into fertile fields. In my American landscape, I wait for the final frost to plant a garden, and as the season erupts with huge vegetables desperate for picking, I go to the orchards to pull fruit with my bare hands, a rebellion against my upbringing.

On Tu b'Shevat, the Jewish new year of the trees, we go to synagogue and eat produce from Israel. Usually it's January or February, and my husband asks why we do this in stark North American winter. *Because Jews celebrate our connection to the land*, I say—a particular and historical land of our long-lived people. We eat dates and olives and pomegranate seeds from the land that holds our heritage, ancestry and memory. The rabbi talks about the symbolism of these fruits—those with a hard outer shell and sweet interior, those which can be eaten whole, those that are edible on the outside but not inside, and then the spiritual symbolism of a mystical fourth fruit that invites contemplation of how land connects to heritage. We sing "Hatikvah," the Israeli national anthem, which means *the hope*. I know the meaning of some of the Hebrew words, especially the ones that refer to the land.

Growing up, we never had a garden. My parents weren't the kind of people who put their hands in the dirt. For a long time, I wanted to know the names of plants. When I bought a home of my own, I planted a garden as a form of rebellion. And also, a coming-home. Each year, I dig up more of the grass and expand the fencing so I can plant vegetables. I bury seeds in soft, spongy soil, water, rake, weed. Tomatoes and cucumbers and leafy greens and zucchinis grow all summer long and into the fall, until the first real frost, and then I carry arms-full of produce flecked with dirt from my little spot of cultivated earth into my secure house. Sometimes I pop a sun-warmed tomato onto my tongue and stab it with my teeth just to feel the spray of juice and seeds in my mouth, sweet and tangy and hot just off the vine.

I don't need a safe room in this part of the world, though we lock our doors and set an alarm for an illusion of protection. Nothing grows here in the winter, but in Israel, the growing season is all year long. Since the war broke out, I've checked flight times and costs. I want to go to pick fruit for the people who aren't there to do it. If fields are abandoned, the economy falters, and the only Jewish state in the world starts to crumble. I can't have that.

But I had a trip in January and another in February and another in March, and there is only so much money. I want to go, but I don't go. I wish I were there. I feel guilty that I'm not. Privileged. So many times I've said *I want to go, I want to help, but I can't or I won't or maybe later.*

I live in the in-between. So Jewish, and so American, living here, while my heart is there. My first time in Israel, just after the assassination of Yitzhak Rabin, something in the air, the soil, made me weep. And the storefronts and restaurants with mezuzahs on their doors—a boutique, a corner grocery, emblazoned with the symbol of a Jewish home. It was the first place I felt I belonged, fully. Everywhere, there were Jews. Beautiful, strong, outspoken and strident. These were my people, finally. Not the shadows of Jews with pale sunken cheeks and striped pajamas. Not bearded brethren hiding behind musty books. Not American immigrants changing their names to better fit in.

When I was young and single and living in a small post-war bungalow alone, I woke many nights in a sweat, shaken by a dream of Cossacks banging at my door. I kept

a hammer under the bed just in case. I can't explain it. I
don't descend from Holocaust survivors, have never endured a pogrom. Maybe it's generational trauma coursing
through my blood. So many generations in the past, but
still there, reminding me to pay attention, to never trust.

In the fall, when we pick apples, one orchard also has
patches of tomatoes and pumpkins and green beans. Egg-
plants and peppers. There was once broccoli and cabbage,
smelly in the lingering heat. We fill bags with apples, pull
Romas and beefsteaks from vines. Pluck beans like long
slender fingers. Twist the spiky stem of pie pumpkins to
free them for roasting later. Take it all home to make something from nothing.

These days, Israel imports more tomatoes than it grows,
and it's an embarrassment for them. But the grape tomatoes, an Israeli invention, are plentiful. In America, I cut
them small and dice cucumber and red onion and red
pepper, mix in parsley and fresh-squeezed lemon juice and
olive oil, salt and pepper, eating my ancestry far from the
land, to feel connected to it.

Five days after Hamas invaded Israel, I called Nedal.
He'd come to Michigan in 2013 as a refugee of the Syrian
civil war. I met him when I was doing PR for a resettle-
ment agency, prepped him for interviews with *US News
& World Report* and *Rolling Stone,* drank Arabic coffee in

a porcelain mug with a cube of sugar melted into it. I've interviewed him on my podcast. I buy pastries from his café. We like each other's Instagram posts.

After October 7, I was posting about Israel. The pain. The attack. The unbearable global Jew-hate. Unabashedly pro-Israel, my posts were fierce. *Hear my pain*, I was crying on social media. *Tell me I'm not alone. Help me make sense of this upside-down world.* He saw them all, and I wondered what he was thinking.

"I was taught to hate Jews," he said. "In school, from the government. Israel was to blame for everything. Then I came here and met you and other Jewish people and realized that was wrong. The only answer is to show love for everyone."

We were five days out from a massacre, and the victims were being blamed for it.

"If Israel goes to war in Gaza, it's just going to create more hate for Israel," he said. This was before the ground invasion, when the war was only an idea. When people were picking through the rubble, trying to identify charred remains.

We knew war was coming—I wanted Israel to eradicate every last terrorist. Make it safe again for all of us. Show the world we won't be wiped off the map. Maintain the image of strong, capable Jews, able to defend themselves from anything.

Then he told a story about how when he moved into his house, his neighbor called the police. Nedal was mowing the lawn too late at night. "I didn't know," he said. "He didn't like me, but I kept saying hello and smiling. Now we are friends." It took two years.

Some people say it's possible for Jews and Arabs to live peacefully side-by-side. I used to agree, but I don't know anymore. People I once called friends are chanting "Free Palestine." As if the real victims are the ones who murdered and raped and beheaded, as if their actions can ever be legitimate forms of protest. The world opposes the Jews, and the little voice inside me is getting louder. *Now you see,* it's saying. *You'll always be different, always be an outsider. You think you can blend, but you can't.*

But rather than get tied up in all the rhetoric, I want to do something tangible, with my hands, in the presence of well-meaning people with big and open hearts. So I keep coming back to the fruit. To the need to grow, to pick, to eat. The universal human need for simple nourishment that is never sated. And the way the Jews transformed Israel from a barren land to an agricultural oasis. I think I fell in love with Israel because it was the first time, the first place, I saw Jews as strong and connected to the land. All the other images of my people didn't inspire me; this one continues to. A Jew who won't be pushed around. A Jew who believes in the beauty of our collective values. A Jew who gets her hands dirty as the sun bakes into her skin.

There are so many dividing lines in the world of people. I used to think we'd moved beyond that, that humans had evolved, but I think it was a dream. A hope. A wish. And then I think of animals who wander in the fields, in the forest, in the jungle, stopping when they're hungry to eat off the branches, crouching to shit in the shade and fertilize the next crop. We are animals who think we are above the animals with our ability to think and reason and plan. But we are the ones leaving the fruit to ferment on the branches, letting the fruit die on the vine.

In February, I text a friend, a master gardener who starts her seeds in the harsh cold of winter. Come spring, her entire yard will be taken up by plants. She is teaching me the names, showing me how to push the seeds into soft and warm soil with my fingers and watch them grow. Even in difficult places, I am learning to grow things year-round.

This essay was first published in GREEN GOLEM MAGAZINE on March 12, 2024. https://greengolemmag.com/2024/03/12/coming-back-to-the-fruit/

14

FIVE DAYS IN ISRAEL DURING A WAR

I srael is beautiful at this time of year. The rolling hills are green and yellow and white, with wild mustard growing at the roadside and daisies opening their eyes under a warming sun. Nights are cool, and days are breathable. My skin pinks as I walk through Tel Aviv, stopping to admire the happy people folk dancing on a Saturday morning and the three elderly men playing violins beside the beach.

This is a country at war, but it's a place filled with people who love the land and the people on it deeply. One night, a man draped in an Israeli flag joined hordes gathered in the center of Tel Aviv to advocate for change. Another night, a little girl in a yellow shirt held a handmade sign at a vigil for the hostages in Modiin.

Everywhere, life is flowing, but there is also emptiness. The wind at the Western Wall plaza echoes. Except for soldiers and school groups, no one is there. Gone, the hordes of tourists who so frequently come to press palms and faces into the ancient stones. I move close to the Kotel, and though I rarely pray, this time I ask God to keep the nation of Israel safe, to unite the Jewish people, to stem the tide of hatred, to bring us all into peace.

Even as war has raged in the aftermath of Hamas's vicious attack on October 7th, a new National Library of Israel opened. It is an impressive building, filled with books about this land, this ancient history, my ancestry, my tradition. On the day I visit, tables are filled with people reading, studying, working. In the front, behind glass, are chairs, one for each hostage still held in Gaza. Below a picture of each person is a book carefully selected to align with their interests. Such care, such devotion, such knowing of the people—where else in the world would that happen?

The Messages I Take Away

When they hear why I've come, people thank me.

"You came just to volunteer? Wow."

I'm glad I could do it, I say. It feels like nothing is more important than this.

A week earlier, I'd led a Rosh Chodesh (new month) writing workshop at my synagogue. This month is Adar, the month when Jews are commanded to increase our happiness.

When the month of Adar enters, we increase in joy. Talmud, Taanit 29a

The Torah defines happiness as celebrating with others and taking care of less-fortunate members of our community.

I went to Israel to help. To see and carry home the truth, to defy the damning headlines. It's a place of great passion and fun, but this time I only wanted to hear people's voices, see what they endure, lend a hand. I picked oranges until my clothes were drenched in sweat and my fingers sliced raw by the branches. Still, the breeze was as sweet as those juicy fruits.

Near the Gaza border, I cut tomatoes into slices for burgers. All the people working at that pop-up were volunteers. They feed 10,000 soldiers a day, from donated food. I sat at a table with a family from Mexico and employees of Bezek, Israel's biggest communications company. Someone put music on a loudspeaker and the song, "Am Yisrael Chai" (the nation of Israel lives) blared out. We started dancing and singing, and the sun was bright and warm, and I almost cried from the joy of it.

At Hostage Family HQ, I lined up plastic yellow ribbons on a piece of posterboard, dropped a dot of glue on each, then pressed in metal pins. These, they sell to raise money for the hostage families' advocacy and so they can sue Hamas in The Hague. I ask everyone at the table to tell me their Aliyah story. One came from Philadelphia, another from London. Another was born here but her family had emigrated a generation earlier from South Africa.

A young woman named Dana volunteers for the Bring Them Home social media team. On October 8th, she quit her job and came to volunteer as part of a 30-person team posting about each hostage so people won't forget them.

My first flight was delayed, and I hardly slept the whole time I was there, but I was happy every moment of this trip. I think I was living the message of the rabbis, about how our tradition defines happiness: to help others, to give to those in need. I have been fortunate all my life to go on vacations that indulge my senses, but those trips contain a lonely kind of emptiness. This trip was all about giving, and I've never been so happy.

Why It Was Important to Go

The day after I returned home, a woman interviewed me for her podcast. She told me she was adopted, and after a DNA test, learned she is half Jewish. Her biological father's surname was Cohn, my maiden name.

"They tell me those were the high priests," she says.

Yes.

In Jerusalem, I bought a necklace bearing the priestly blessing. I am a daughter of a cohain, I carry this blessing through generations, back to the time of the Temple.

Jews have called this land holy for thousands of years. I pressed my palms into the soft stones of the last standing wall of the Temple. Some call it the Wailing Wall, to connote the sadness of having our holy place destroyed. I prayed beside soldiers in khaki skirts and religious women in wigs, all of us eyes-closed, leaning into hope.

On Shabbat, at a writer-friend's table, we introduced ourselves by name, place of origin and reason we were there. One person said, "I'm here because I'm Jewish." Another said, "I'm here because I'm a Zionist." I said, "I'm here to volunteer and be a witness."

On Sunday I participated in a writers workshop about place. Start your stories with the place, the instructor said. The sand on the sidewalk. The way barren cracked land is now green with trees. The sharp taste of the wild mustard at the roadside. The juice of a ripe orange soaking my chin.

Driving to Jerusalem, my guide said, "That's your tree over there," pointing to a grove planted over decades by Jewish National Fund. American Jews like me grew up putting coins, *tzedakah*, in little blue boxes at Hebrew school to plant trees in the land of Israel. Our contribution to our ancestral land has turned it verdant and productive, thriving and giving.

I went to be there for my brethren, but I went for myself, too. To remind me of who I am. Since October 7th, I've been wearing my star of David necklaces, proudly exhibiting my Jewish identity. I'm pulled to be among people who get it, who feel what I feel, all the complicated emotions of this trying time.

In Israel, every door has a mezuzah slanting against the lintel. Stores. Cafés. Hotels. In the taxi on the way to the airport on my last night, the driver, whose name was Shay, like my son, Shaya, said, "You should make Aliyah. Soon. Before Passover, if you can." Aliyah means to ascend, and it's the word used to refer to Diaspora Jews who emigrate to Israel.

I wish, I said and laughed. *That's a month from now.*

"It's important," he said. He was young, the father of a three-year-old. His parents came from Iraq and Egypt because there was nowhere else they could go.

"We have to pray," he said. He looked like he belonged in a nightclub. No yarmulke. Tight shirt. Fitted jeans. His skin was Middle Eastern dark, his hair cropped close. He didn't look like someone who invokes prayer, but he

encouraged me to beseech God to protect us, to bring all
the Jews together, to keep us strong, to keep us safe, and I
nodded along.

What It Means to Be a Witness

At the site of the Nova music festival, pictures of the 364
killed and 44 kidnapped stand where they were dancing
before being gunned down. Parents, friends, family members have personalized the memorials. One mother wrote
about how special her son was. I couldn't stop the tears. It
could've been my sons. It could've been me.

Signs said, *When you get home, dance forever. If I don't
come home, know I love you. Zachinu l'ehov: we had the
chance to love.*

I visited the car cemetery. That's what they're calling
the place where all the burned cars were brought. Charred
rusty hulks of former vehicles are stacked, and those not
entirely destroyed are parked as if in a lot, a carpool spot,
except no one is coming back.

As for the cars that had people in them when set ablaze,
where the people melted into the metal, the car was buried
with the humans. Jews believe every piece of a human
is precious. We comb massacre sites—remnants of a bus

bombing, the aftermath of a terrorist attack—for any piece of flesh to bury it properly.

We ate lunch in Sderot, a town close to Gaza where terrorists destroyed the police station. On October 7th, thousands flooded across the border. They knew where to go because they'd spent years planning this attack, posing as friends, workers building houses for peace-loving Israelis, all the while collecting information, the people trusting them, believing peace was possible despite borders and barriers.

People just want to live. It's not a Jewish thing. But this constant focus on life, on living, on lifting up and seeing the humanity in another, that is a Jewish value. It's so deep, it's part of our DNA.

My last stop before flying home was Hostage Square. Opposite the building where the War Cabinet meets daily, this open plaza is filled with artistic statements.

- A gallows with Hebrew words saying: Time Is Up.

- A long table with seats for every person still captive. Half a pita, bottles of dirty water, to represent what they are given to eat.

- A tunnel to mimic what it's like underground. It

was scary to walk through, but we emerged into the light. When will they?

- A butterfly beneath a net, symbolizing the freedom they yearn for.

- A tent with bound and bloodied legs sticking out of it.

- So many paintings with poetic statements and colorful multimedia displays.

Members of the attacked kibbutzim described what it was like to live there, how much peace was in the hearts of the residents.

"It's like a bad dream you can't wake up from," one woman said. "You can't believe it's real."

I met a woman who made Aliyah forty years ago. All those years, she was never scared. Not when rockets rained down nor when sirens blared. Now, she's scared. It's an existential fright, a fear we don't know what to do with, can't find our way out of.

But on Shabbat morning, I watched Israelis folk-dance. Three elderly men played violins on the sidewalk. Young families kicked up sand; teens played volleyball and surfed. Religious couples strolled along the sea. Life went on. Because it has to. Because we must cherish the moments we have. Israelis get this. When will the rest of the world?

This essay was first published in THE TIMES OF IS-RAEL on March 28, 2024. https://blogs.timesofisrael.com /five-days-in-israel-during-a-war/

15

— · —

HOW I STAY CLOSE TO MY SON WHILE ARGUING OVER ISRAEL AND PALESTINE

"I owe you an apology, Mom. I didn't give you enough credit."

My nineteen-year-old son Asher had just listened to an episode of my podcast, in which I interviewed a Palestinian and an Israeli, both living in the West Bank, who were working with an organization called Roots to figure out how to coexist.

I am a pro-Israel progressive, so when my pro-BDS son wants to discuss Israel-Palestine, we often descend into heated debate, Asher referencing articles or advocacy groups, while I recount my journalistic experiences in the Middle East—interviewing Israelis and Arabs, visiting military bases, sidestepping landmines in the Golan Heights, combing every inch of the land to learn its stories.

My eldest son has always enjoyed a good argument—the substance of the debate as much as the energy of the back-and-forth. Since he started college, his lefty politics shifted toward socialist-communist-anarchist. Still, he followed his apology with the words, *I think we're closer on this issue than I realized.*

I knew exactly which part of the podcast changed Asher's perspective. Early in, I referenced the Israeli-Palestinian "conflict" and Noor A'wad, my Palestinian guest, corrected me. "A conflict is a situation where both parties have equal power," he explained. "This is not the case."

I thanked him, and we discussed the importance of using the right words to properly guide the conversation.

I share Asher's dedication to achieving fair treatment and equal access for all people. I believe both Jews and Palestinians are in need of these things, while he believes Palestinians need greater advocacy than Jews in Israel at present. He sees Israel as an ominous oppressor while I see it as a saving grace after centuries of persecution against Jews.

At first, I worried that through these debates, he wouldn't see me as someone to rely on, to trust, to believe in; he feared I was closed-minded, maybe even bigoted.

My children's father is an Orthodox Jew whose sister lives over the Green Line in a religious settlement. With him, they've seen Israel as a spiritual home. I've tried to show them Israel as a place where Jews are strong and accepted without question. Asher doesn't believe Jews need a special place. I do. I emphasize all the good Israel does (if not in its own backyard)—sending rescue teams after earthquakes in Nepal or when the Miami condo collapsed last year, and innovating in science and technology for global benefit, as examples.

Growing up in the 80s, I met Holocaust survivors at school and in my community and draped a tallit over empty chairs on the synagogue bimah to remember Soviet refuseniks. I experienced antisemitism myself—when a boyfriend's father complained that a waiter was "Jewing" him, my boyfriend told him not to say that in front of me instead of telling him not to say it at all.

On my first visit to Israel, when my suitcase didn't arrive, I shopped on Shabbat in East Jerusalem. Weeks after the assassination of Yitzhak Rabin, I was there to write about the death of a dream. I interviewed an Arab shop owner who said Jews and Arabs were friends.

On my next visit, I sat beside a thirty-year-old Palestinian on the plane who was going to visit relatives in Ramallah. For ten hours, we talked about the many things we had in common. *What is this hate about*? I asked; we had no answers. When we landed, he was searched and patted down, because of his dark skin and the name on his passport, while I was *welcomed home* by the customs official, though I have never lived in Israel.

I spent Shabbat in an Old City hostel, kindling tea lights and joining the waterfall of sweeping skirts to the Western Wall as the sun set. I visited family friends who had made Aliyah from Britain. Growing up in the shadow of the Holocaust, I reveled in Israel's strong, confident image of Jews.

My children hear about Israel as bully, occupier from the biased media. Asher uses words like apartheid and genocide. For me, Israel is a dream-come-true, a place where my people have power. I say Israel is the most mis-understood nation on earth, but my kids don't feel op-pressed. They don't feel their heritage is connected to a na-tion halfway around the world. They believe being Jewish is a choice. I know it's not.

I often ask Asher why he devotes such a disproportion-ate amount of energy to this one place. He says it's because Israel is a powerful country that I support without ques-tion. He scrutinizes other countries but doesn't engage me in arguments because we agree on most other places, like our shared concern for the Uyghur Muslims in China. He focused on Israel because he still appreciates his Jewish heritage, even if he doesn't accept all its conflicts.

Initially, I felt rejected, threatened. If my son vilified the only Jewish nation on the planet, had I failed to instill

Jewish values in my children? And what did his vilifying say about how he saw me and my unwavering support for Israel?

But he doesn't view our disagreement as a threat. "When you're close with someone," he told me, "you don't get to lay out your argument and walk away, mic drop. You have to engage. There needs to be a respectful back and forth."

I agreed, and I like to think I taught him that. I also taught him to speak his mind and stand up for right over wrong. We raise our children to see things more clearly than we do. I tried to enlighten my parents on race and privilege. And now Asher is teaching me to listen, to confront my inconsistencies and blind spots.

I've offered to travel with him so we can visit the West Bank, hear perspectives of people on the ground. He says, "Sure, someday." At least he's not saying no. Our relationship is lifelong, and there is time to deepen this conversation by gathering more information to expand our perspectives.

In his second year at St. Olaf College, preparing to sing in the Christmas concert, Asher felt conspicuous as one of the few Jewish students on the Lutheran campus. He'd sung in plenty of holiday concerts before, but this was religious, with only one faith story told and all the participants buying into a narrow perspective.

So he wore a kippah with his choir robe. Now, he wears it every day. Our stances can change as we encounter more situations and reflect on them. I hope that will happen with my son on the matter of Israel. He hopes that for me, too. At least I know we'll keep talking, and that's the most important thing.

A version of this essay first appeared in THE FORWARD on February 15, 2022, https://forward.com/opinion/482522/how-i-stay-close-to-my-son-while-arguing-over-israel-and-palestine/

TELL ME SOMETHING NEW

16

LOVING THE LANDSCAPE

We'd been in the new house just a few days the first time it snowed that year. The kids were small, and we tromped out into the sleepy world, our footsteps marring the expansive blanket of gleaming white. We packed snowballs in our mittened palms and lobbed them across the yard. After, we fell onto the foot-deep heaps to make angels with our arms and legs. And when we came in from the cold, our cheeks were red from the minty air, our souls quieted by the sparkling day.

All of this was mine—the trees like sentries, the sculpted bushes that in warmer months bore roses. There was so much space, more than I had imagined when we quickly toured the century-old abode and pledged to buy it for more than we could comfortably spend. It would be good for the children to live in a neighborhood of families, we reasoned, and made the numbers make sense so we could have a home in a coveted neighborhood along Detroit's first ring of suburbs.

So many of my firsts came later in my life. Like, I was middle-aged when I first went on a winter hike. There is something breathtaking and reverent about the quiet that accompanies the cold. It beckons me from couch-side hibernation to discover a world few ever see. InMichigan, there are 150 days of sun and they're disproportionately in the warmer months, but sometimes, there's a perfect winter day with bright sun that gleams off the snow. Once, when it was eighteen degrees Fahrenheit with new snow two feet deep, I trekked out into the quiet drifts. The fresh snow sparkled, and I didn't mind the cold. I trailed along a ridge, down into a valley, alongside a frozen pond and up through a leafless forest, just to witness the winter. Eventually, warm from the effort, I arrived back where I began, exhilarated by doing something most never try.

In my new home, the sun backlit icy tree branches and transformed the snow into a sea of tiny diamonds. I remember the branches reaching. I remember the snow fluffy and white, the trees dark and skeletal.

One morning, a red fox sat on the brick wall at the back of our yard. The satin of her copper fur matched the rough red of the bricks. We stared at her out the window before leaving for school and work. The cold seeped into my bones, became a hollow wind in my chest, and I wondered where she would go. Was there a den nearby with babies waiting for the warmth of their mother, or was she a lone wanderer stuck in the suburbs with no one to claim her?

Eventually, the snow melted and summer came to the new house. Ivy covered the brick. We explored the yard, tore out the rose bushes to plant a vegetable garden. There was a pond with cracks webbed into the foundation, so we filled it with dirt and bricks and scattered tiny stones over the top. Once, sitting on the soil, pulling weeds, sweat beading on my face under a hot sun, my daughter saw a baby deer lying in the shade on top of the old pond. We fell quiet against the rapid conversation of birds. The ferns behind the garage were matted down from where the mama had laid to push her baby out on a clear summer night, against a soundtrack of pulsing crickets. I remember the white spots on the baby's soft fur and how my other daughter ran to the house for carrots, but I stopped her and herded the kids inside to give the mother space to return for her baby. Sweat trickled in rivers along my skin. It was so still I could almost feel the baby's heart pulsing beneath its soft fur. An hour later, it was gone.

A friend called. "It's too hot to do anything," she moaned.

People complain about Michigan weather. They say winter is too cold and lasts too long, while summer is too humid and fleeting. Everyone loves the brief fall except for the bees in the apple orchards. Spring is a memory before it begins. I planned my second wedding for June 4th, anticipating a day of bright sun and mild temperatures. But it was so hot and sticky that the kids jumped into the lake in their clothes after the ceremony. The best pictures from that day are of the kids' faces, crystal droplets of lake water highlighting their eyes.

Across from my house, there is a public golf course. People roll carts and shoulder bags over the lilting hills. A fence surrounds it, and families of deer live inside it. Maybe the fox, too. The golf course abuts the zoo, and the people who live near it can hear the lions roar at night. On July fourth, fireworks explode over the golf course and the animals go crazy. The environmentalists in my neighborhood protest every year, but people come from miles around to watch the night sky painted with color, so nothing changes.

During the pandemic, my only solace was walking around the neighborhood, waving to neighbors, eyes bright with the desire to come close. One day in that terrible time of grounded planes and face masks and people dying in hospitals filled to bursting, I saw the fox. She pawed along a driveway, her fur clumpy and knotted. She'd clearly seen better days. And she was alone, as before. I worried that she wasn't doing well. The world was quiet. We were baking bread and making complicated meals in the middle of the day, the kids doing school on their computers, and my husband working at home. Too many of us in this house at once, but it was reassuring to be all together.

It's been years now since I've seen the fox. I've imagined her silky pelt and magic eyes as she ducks under decks, hides in shrubs. Perhaps emerged from a near forest, stunned by the brightness of the built world, and meandered along our streets with curiosity. I liked the idea of a fox in my neighborhood, as if we were more than just an American suburb.

Foxes are known for their cunning. But their biggest predator, it turns out, is humans. In London, there are 10,000 foxes screeching at night. They are deft, elegant, beautiful. Bushy tails and gleaming pelts, triangular ears and keen eyes. They live on every continent but Antarctica. The screaming happens before they mate, not during, a warning cry, a signal that something big is about to happen. But I've never heard it here.

The word *fox* means thick-haired or tail, and the female is a vixen. A group of foxes is a skulk, a leash or an earth, but honestly, I only ever dealt with one lone fox in this square-mile town. Perhaps that was the problem, why she was so bedraggled the last time we crossed paths. Few creatures do well on their own.

The deer visit often, and the rabbits multiply with great regularity in burrows beneath the grass of my yard. They are not afraid of me nor hampered by human traffic. They come and they come, and I make room for them, as I would for that lone fox, should she perch on my brick wall ever again.

It's a choice to love your landscape. When the snow is inches thick on the branches, I marvel at its balance. Ice claws around the thinnest part of the wood, the snow like lace or cotton or a grandfather's beard. The ground lifts in waves. And then the summer comes, and everything is lush and fragrant and my garden overflows with zucchini and tomatoes. I like to think we all need each other to survive. The intricate geometric displays of this landscape are the quiet after the storm, which is its own kind of beautiful, for anyone who can see it.

17

—·—

LUXURY OR NECESSITY

Every Christmas Day, I clean out the basement—pulling out plastic totes and riffling through to see what we can toss, dusting off books and games, mopping behind the couch, categorizing and organizing the stuff we've hidden away for later. I look forward to this with great enthusiasm, but my husband and four nearly grown children do not. They surrender to my demands but wish I would forget this ritual. But when I clear things out, I can breathe again, like a weight has lifted off my hunched shoulders. I have space to think. I keep waiting for them to feel it, too.

Every room of my 2,500-square-foot house is filled with stuff. Photographs and paintings cover walls and counters, and all manner of bric-a-brac clutter surfaces. Just the other day, I removed several of my kids' canvas creations from the basement wall and tossed them in the garbage outside. They were mostly the abstract swipes of color that young children call art. With no idea who did which painting and no claim from my kids, it was time for them to go.

When I was a child and wanted something in a store, my mother would ask, "Is it a luxury or a necessity?"

I took this question seriously, for my mother was always serious. If I truly needed something, she would buy it. But if there was an inkling of want behind the request, well, then perhaps we could simply walk on and reserve the desire for another day, or never.

We went through my closet twice a year, spring and fall, the seasons when new clothes replaced those I outgrew. "If you haven't worn it in a year, it goes," Mom insisted.

When I moved away, she came to wherever I was living and offered the same service. Mom discouraged me from shopping at mark-down knock-off stores to get a good deal because they usually carried clothing no one wanted and that matched nothing.

"If you don't know what you'll wear it with, you'll never wear it," she said. "Buy outfits, not pieces."

So many times, I bought a shirt that I loved but could not figure out what to pair it with, so it remained on a hanger, often with tags on, until I dumped it in a bag of clothes to donate.

When my father died, my mother opened drawers and cupboards to find them overflowing with long-forgotten papers of Dad's long-shuttered company, rubber bands and paper clips grown so brittle they snapped in half, remote controls and cords that attached to machines long gone from the house. Dad died two months before the pandemic, so my grieving mother, alone in the home they built when I was a baby, distracted herself from the rising case counts by clearing out Dad's junk. She filled double-thick Heftys with all the stuff she didn't want—which was all the stuff—and left them in various upstairs rooms for my husband and sons to lug to the curb. Whenever she thought she had finished, she discovered another drawer or shelf crowded with useless junk.

I'll never understand why my father held onto it all. His bulk purchases always seemed practical: two or three bottles of shampoo, multiple bars of soap, family-sized tubes of toothpaste, huge packages of toilet paper. It was important to have "backup," he said, which seemed like good planning. Dad wasn't a particularly materialistic person, and he cared little for clothing. My mother guided his fashion decisions, telling him when it made sense to buy a tuxedo and ushering him away from the kelly green pants.

Both of my parents grew up with modest means. Dad's father, my grandpa Sid, drove a milk delivery truck along the streets of Detroit. Grandma Sarah didn't work, and they lived a quiet life in a small house. Once, Dad showed me the three places he'd lived as a boy—one was an empty lot, the other two overrun with graffiti and broken windows. He recalled how his mother sent him at age six to the bar on the corner to bring his father home for dinner and how, as a teen, he got into street fights when kids made antisemitic comments.

Mom's childhood was more protected. Grandpa Artie, her father, cared more what the neighbors thought than what was truly needed. But he had little career success as a job-hopping bookkeeper and there were appearances to keep up, so his debonair, beloved father-in-law, my great-grandfather, Grandpa Louie, made sure Mom and her siblings had everything they wanted.

I imagine Grandpa Artie's childhood home was sparse. His parents were Polish immigrants, with seven children on New York's Lower East Side. They likely lived in a tenement, and I've seen those two- or three-room apartment walkups where kids slept on floors and in corners because there weren't enough beds or even space to hold them. Grandpa believed he deserved bigger things, and once grown, he lived like it. I learned later that people were always bailing him out—my aunts and uncles, my own parents, a wealthy cousin. So perhaps her father's overspending made my mother the practical one and my father's family frugality made him a collector who couldn't let go. If you had asked me years ago, before my father became sick with acute myeloid leukemia and then died from it, I would have said that my mother was the materialistic one and my father the one who could live on nothing, by himself, near no one. I would have been wrong.

In clothing stores, Mom always intoned, "Luxury or necessity?" That is how I learned to love thrifting, finding new life for cast-offs that cost no more than $10 or $20. And I think long and hard before making a purchase.

But clothing always disappoints me. I expect transformation with the feel of a fabric or the look of an outfit, yet the reality falls short. The cloth doesn't hug my curves or caress my shoulders. The pants are too tight at the waist. The shirt sleeves shrink in the wash, and the colors fade. Mom taught me to be happy with what I have, not to think that a new item will somehow make my life better. I don't own a lot of clothing. I am careful, now, with those acquisitions because I realize their limitations.

In contrast, I have way too many books, in every single room. That's because when I was young, my father took me to bookstores and said, "Anything you want, Lynnie! Books are knowledge, and you can never have enough." I can't seem to let go of the strong spines or careful words, even though I rarely reread them. I survey my packed shelves with titles not cracked in decades, pledging to pull them down but never actually doing so. I rationalize that books are a comfort: brilliant revelations surrounding me, words to discover, stories that might change how I see myself.

But if I don't read them over and over, what good do they serve? I could gain equal insight and wisdom from library books, borrowed, cherished, then shared with another patient soul. Holding on may be my way of keeping my father alive. But as I think back on those dusty months when my mother dug out all the forgotten items from the hollows of her home, I know I don't want my legacy to be that I couldn't let go of the past.

I live in a nice house in an old city with walls painted deep, rich hues—peacock blue in the living room, royal purple in the family room, warm brown in the basement. Everywhere filled with furniture and rugs, tables and bookshelves and a piano my mother-in-law shipped from Washington, D.C. that is rarely played. The closets are full of old coats.

The kids are leaving now, moving into their own lives. The rooms will soon whisper with echoes. And while I love this place where we melded into a family after heartbreak and divorce and remarriage and blending, I am ready to leave it, to say goodbye to what I no longer need and choose a small and cozy spot, with tall trees and land to walk on, near to a river or a forest where I can contemplate what really matters.

Luxury is defined as "great comfort and extravagant living," while necessity is about being required, indispensable. True comfort is a deep and abiding love, even in the throes of anger or frustration, and the knowledge that my days matter and my nights endure.

My real treasures are a dog-eared cookbook I inherited from my grandmother and the tiny black and white photos of my parents as children—more precious than the tufted velvet Arhaus couch that I never sit on or the crystal vases growing dusty from neglect.

I don't need a big house to be happy. When my youngest graduates from high school, I'll find a quiet place, with just enough space. My husband and I will donate most of our belongings and take only what we really need: a couple sturdy sweaters, my favorite blankets, the comforter with the little leaves that keeps us warm on the coldest nights. A set of skillets and two deep pots, to make soup or pasta. One good knife. Over the years, I've collected mugs from my travels and filled a closet with cookbooks, but I'll take only a few favorites, the ones I actually use.

And as for the boxes of memories in the basement, I will summon the courage to let them go, like my mother taught me. We rarely return to cramped storage units and crowded corners anyway, leaving them for others to wade through after your life is done, the most unwelcome gift. It is a luxury to keep things for which you have no use, not even remember you own. The real necessity is to live simply and well while you can.

This essay first appeared in BIOSTORIES on January 4, 2023, https://biostories.com/wp-content/uploads/2023/01/Luxury-or-Necessity.pdf

18

— · —

PROM DRESS IN A PANDEMIC

"Butterfly dresses are the thing, Mom," Eliana whispered. "Can you imagine if I went to prom in a butterfly dress?"

It was long and beaded, the blue of a shimmering pool. Sequin butterflies fluttered in bursts of color, one the deep golden of my daughter's hair.

We were one mother-daughter pair of a dozen mother-daughter pairs in a tiny shop stuffed with racks of dresses pressed together so tightly it was hard to see each one. The proprietor kept track of the number of people in the store, as impatient women and girls waited outside in the lingering cold of late winter. Inside, we were masked and trying to distance, but urgency seemed to overshadow pandemic protocols: We hoped our teens would have their magical night. After a year of disappointment, death, painful politics and online school from stuffy bedrooms, we were desperate for a happy ending.

Still, I hadn't wanted to go dress shopping. I'd been struggling to relate to my daughter's desperation for senior year excitement and glamor. For a month before our shopping date, she lashed out because I wouldn't let her go to Florida for spring break: "I won't die fromCOVID! But I'll never have another senior year." From our suburban home, as snowy wind swept the streets in clouds, she watched friends post pictures from beaches and parties. When her friends came home with COVID, I thought I'd be vindicated. But I wasn't.

Eliana kept doing all the things kids do to become independent—insisting she knew best, chafing at having to follow my rules, rolling her eyes. She saw me as out-of-touch, as if I'd never been a teenage girl. Granted, I'd never been a teen in a pandemic, but it felt frivolous to want special occasions and expensive dresses as hospitals overflowed with patients gasping their last breaths, their families robbed of the chance to say goodbye.

The lack of generosity I felt toward my daughter didn't gel with my vision of myself as a mother. All I'd wanted was to birth babies, hold them close and raise them to feel so loved they'd never grow distant. But I was having a hard time letting go.

***

My sweet little girl slipped out in two pushes before my midwife could get to the birthing center. The next morning, she lay on the bed beside me while her father walked to synagogue to name her Eliana, Hebrew for "God answers," Greek for "daughter of the sun."

Eliana was the insistent newborn who stayed awake until late and slept until long after dawn's golden fingers gripped the day. She was the toddler who insisted I rock her at two a.m., the five-year-old who asked me to remove the training wheels from her bicycle and rode off in perfect balance. She was the child who never flinched when the nurse poked her with needles, the little girl who, before attending school, exclaimed, "I wrote my name!" and when I looked at the paper, there were those six letters, scribbled in crayon, with confidence.

She loved frills and tulle and pink and purple, layered strings of beads around her neck, painted her nails and preferred decorative ponytails for her silky hair. Eliana's cake pops won the neighborhood baking contest the first time she entered, at age ten. Now, at eighteen, she expertly applies a full face of makeup, looks impeccably beautiful in Doc Martens, ripped jeans and oversized sweaters, stunning even in sweatpants. My sweet girl, my tough girl, my strong girl. She came from me, but she has never been of me—confident where I doubt myself, remarkably immune to criticism. For the first three decades of my life, I cared inordinately what people thought, longing for praise from family members, friends, teachers, even passers-by. My daughter is discerning about whose opinions affect her—select friends', her stepsister's, mine.

I admire her toughness, but sometimes it perplexes me. While my sons are sweet and snuggly, Eliana has a mind and mission of her own. Like me, she is defiant, and sometimes I don't do right by her. I regret words I've uttered in the heat of mother-daughter battle—accusing her of not caring about others' feelings, of focusing only on herself. When I was growing up, I felt my mother rarely listened to me; I believed she didn't see the real me. I never wanted a child of mine to feel the sting of silence.

***

1989: Our hair is big, our clothing bright neon. In shoulder pads and two-tone shoes, blue eye shadow and shiny lips, we are telling the world we are here; we don't need coiffures and ironed clothes, tucked shirts or slick haircuts.

Back then, I always had a boyfriend but never believed I was lovable. I was too much for everyone—strong, intense, speaking my mind. I stood on the outskirts of popular, with friends in every clique, never belonging to one. How my family saw me influenced how I saw myself. Instead of calling me *strong* or *a leader*, they said I was *bossy* and had a *big mouth*. I vowed that when I became a mother, I would never discredit a daughter of mine for sharing opinions or defying societal expectations. I would love my daughter so much that she'd always believe in herself.

I went to prom every year of high school, and each time my mother bought me a pretty dress for under $100. But for my senior prom, she spent $500 on a snow-white strapless number with fitted bodice and peplum layers—a dress everyone would remember.

"It's your senior prom," she rationalized.

I imagined walking in and everyone looking up, holding their breath at the sight of me, my curly hair blown straight, sparkly eye shadow and glossy lipstick illuminating my face. They'd smile, nod in approval. Someone might whisper, "Did you see Lynne's dress?" I would overhear, of course, and hold that moment as my high school grand finale.

Instead, five other girls, including the prom queen, showed up in my $500 dress.

***

Eliana buzzed among long dresses in a rainbow of fabrics

and colors. The first row held poofy gowns. The second offered sequins and beads. Beyond that hung shorter dresses, which Eliana insisted were not prom length, and the far wall showcased a mishmash of styles—black-tie dressy, two-piece ensembles, ball gowns with strapless bodices.

She wanted something straight and form-fitting with subtle embellishment. The salesgirl surveyed Eliana's pink satin minidress, cropped sweater, white Doc Martens boots, and little red handbag. She had straightened her hair, applied wings at the corners of her eyes. Her nails were long and manicured.

"I have to show you this." She led us to a plastic-covered sheath. The butterfly dress.

We were browsing expensive, final-sale gowns, hoping our girls would have a chance to wear them. So far, the plan at Eliana's school was to hold prom at an empty farmers' market. Masks required, no sit-down meal, no dates from other schools.

My senior year had been grand, with a formal homecoming, full-contact powder puff football game, prom and graduation and an all-night party with blackjack, a bounce house and door prizes. For spring break, my parents sent me on an unchaperoned Caribbean cruise. My daughter had been stuck at home all year with only me for company. I loved all this bonus time with my kids, but for them, spending day and night with me was no longer enough.

Of course, teens are supposed to grow up and spread their wings, develop identities and ambitions and lives of their own. The pandemic highlighted how much I loved being with them, how in awe I am of my nearly adult children, and how hard it would be to see them go.

***

By the time she stepped into the butterfly dress, Eliana and I were on our third store. In every shop, she had tried on stunning gowns but hadn't found "the one."

As Eliana slipped into the delicate beaded gown, the saleswoman and I held our collective breath. This dress was so intricate, unique and different. I wanted it to fit. Eliana's senior year had started in lockdown and stayed that way until March. We barred mask-averse friends from our home. For a time when things looked really bad, we barred everyone. After a year of nothing, prom was every-thing to Eliana, and I wanted to make it perfect for her.

In normal times, a prom dress is a farewell, the dress you hope people remember you in—*if* they remember you. The dress you recall when you've grown thick around the middle and your hair has thinned and you're not sure if you want to attend your reunion. All your hopes and dreams for your life wrapped up in a piece of fabric, the boning of the bodice, the intricate lacework.

But in a pandemic, a prom dress is a symbol of freedom. A transformation from nightmare to dream.

The beaded fabric skimmed her slim curves; delicate straps hovered on her satin skin. Her eyes sparkled. She'd found her dress.

When I turned the tag over and saw that it cost $700, my stomach clenched. It was so far beyond what I'd imagined spending. But I took a deep breath and pulled out my wallet.

"Are you sure, Mom?" Eliana said. "It's so expensive."

"I'm sure," I said.

I bought the dress as an apology for not being enough and for being too much, an attempt to erase all our stupid fights. I bought the dress to show my deep and abiding love for my daughter and to compensate for how my imperfect parenting might have sent a different message.

Was this why my mother spent so much on my dress all those years ago? To cling to me? To win my favor? To buy a reprieve from our incessant fighting? In spending an unconscionable sum, did she hope that I'd view her with compassion, that we'd turn a corner in our relationship? Had she, too, planned to be a different kind of mother and, in the final hour, worry that she'd failed?

***

Prom happened on a May evening. Among 350 class-mates, Eliana was the only one in a butterfly dress. She posed for pictures, including one with me. Then we all trouped to Prom Park, a gathering place in our neighbor-hood, where residents gaze at dresses, tuxedos, up-dos and electric smiles. My mother came, huddling close.

"Look," I said, pointing to a boy in a gold and black tuxedo with ruffled shirt and wingtips.

"So chic," Mom said.

A girl strolled by in a curve-hugging satin sheath. "Ele-gant," we agreed.

They posed for selfies—one girl wore a men's suit, another a red ballgown, still another displayed sparkling sneakers beneath a sleek dress.

"I love how each kid has their own style," I said.

Mom nodded. "They have such a strong sense of self."

"I'm really glad you're here," I said.

"Me, too."

Eliana waved, seeming to hover off the ground. The butterflies glistened in the sun. They'd appeared in our lives fully formed, skipping the difficult metamorphosis of stumbling child to bright-winged adult. I watched my beautiful daughter as she inched away, eager to take flight.

This essay first appeared in QUIBBLE LIT on October 3, 2022, https://www.quibblelit.com/prom-dress-by-lynne-gol odner

19

LOSING THE TRUCK

"Mom," my teenage son whispered late one night. "I think someone just hit my truck."

I lifted my head from the pillow to gaze at his tall shadow in the doorway. Shaya, my baby, seventeen and lanky with dark-brown hair and tortoiseshell glasses.

I hadn't been fully asleep, but I hadn't heard the smash and scrape of one car hitting another either. I nudged my husband awake then shuffled downstairs in black-watch-plaid flannel pants and a T-shirt.

It was a cool night and quiet. The faint whisper of a near highway whooshed through the darkness. The sky was milky gray, a few stars glistening.

"It's not your fault, honey," I said, "but why was your car on the street?"

Shaya's old red Chevy S10 mini truck had been hit so hard it was pushed backwards in front of our driveway. The grill was smashed and dangling. Glass shards glinted in the streetlight and among the wet grass.

"I forgot to move it," he said.

We were a six-person, five-car family, nothing unusual in metro Detroit, the city of cars. And this wasn't the first vehicle left on the street overnight, despite a neighborhood rule to park in driveways.

We live in a square-mile, all-residential town north of Detroit, with old homes and paved roads and strict rules governing the order of the community. Whoever hit the truck had been driving on the wrong side of the road at full speed.

Soon enough, police headlights slowed in front of the house. A young officer surveyed the devastation, scribbled in his notebook.

"This is going to cost thousands to fix," I muttered as we circled the wreckage.

"It's a total loss, ma'am," the officer corrected.

We'd had the truck for eight months. Built in 2003, it had 106,000 miles on it and a jump seat. It fishtailed easily on open highways, despite sandbags holding down the bed. We'd bought it from a seventy-five-year-old man who reminded me of my father, which made it easy for me to ignore the vehicle's condition.

And anyway, he'd offered a pages-thick mechanic report vouching for the vehicle's good form. I know little about cars and I was missing my father, so I chose to believe him. I didn't take the car for a look in an auto shop I trusted. The man was kind, dressed in a sweater and pressed jeans, his white hair neatly brushed and the cars in his garage clean and cared for. I handed over six thousand dollars, cash, and my son was over-the-moon happy. The truck suited him.

But a month later, our sweet red ride required $1,500 of repairs and a month after that, another four-figure sum. I felt stupid.

Thankfully, we passed a few months without a visit to the shop, ignoring the rust above the front left tire (what my mechanic calls "car cancer"). Then the suspension needed replacing, and I insisted I was done.

Shaya asked a handy friend to do the work; we'd buy the parts and pay him for the labor in pizza.

But before we could do anything, a driver totaled the truck in the middle of the night, leaving a heap of metal and glass and a brokenhearted boy.

Shaya had named her Candy, folding his long legs to climb inside and proudly cart around his friends. He zipped into the driveway at the end of a long school day, wearing a perpetual smile behind the wheel.

Since he was a baby, Shaya has given the best hugs. He'd lay his head on my shoulder and pat my back with his tiny hands, reassuring me instead of the other way around.

He's always glowed with smiles, and now, as he towers over me and everyone in our family, I love to lean in and feel his arms close around me.

"I'm so sorry, honey," I said in the middle of that cold night. The front grill hung clear off the truck, a gaping maw, the redness of the paint like blood oozing under the glare of streetlights. He leaned into my arms, and this time, I patted his back.

The officer had said the driver was either drunk or texting. The insurance company confirmed that we were not to blame, declared it a total loss, calculated the value, and sent money to my bank account.

We live a mile away from the first paved thoroughfare in the United States, Woodward Avenue. Every August, classic and vintage cars zoom up and down for the Woodward Dream Cruise. Car lovers come from across America in amped-up chrome and bright paint, taillights like eyes and fancy grills. Detroiters drag lawn chairs to the roadside to sit and watch, sometimes wandering among parking lots of cruisers, gazing under open hoods and talking about times gone by.

Candy wasn't a classic, but she had character. We didn't have enough time with her to learn her stories or create new ones.

In my twenties, I survived two car accidents in a span

of three weeks, both while stopped at a red light. One car hit me from behind, the other head-on. I couldn't have prevented either crash, and both times, the vehicles were a total loss.

For weeks, I had visions of a car racing toward me. I talked to a therapist so I could get back to driving with ease. Detroit is a city of drivers. Even our houses are built with the cars in mind, garages jutting out in front of the architecture. There's little public transportation, few places in easy walking distance.

Back then, I was becoming religious, so I called my rabbi for support.

"It's not a sign from God," he said.

I wanted to believe that it was. A wakeup call, perhaps, a higher power shaking me alert.

But sometimes, there's no easy explanation for the end of something. Shaya lost the truck on a calm night, an ordinary Thursday. The street was quiet, the residents asleep in their beds.

I could say it's a sign to appreciate what you have while you have it. To be grateful my kid wasn't in the truck when it was hit. To thank the gleaming stars in the night sky that this was the worst thing we'd endure that week or that month or that year.

But that doesn't erase the sadness. Maybe it's a reminder

that there's nothing I can do about most things, that power and control are just illusions.

"I miss her," Shaya said a few days later. I knew how he felt, despite how frivolous and privileged it felt to mourn the loss of an old, old truck.

20

BEFORE I LEAVE YOU

Paddling into the lifting waves, a constant current rolling in and sucking out, I hefted across two-and-a-half miles of lively ocean with my daughter, though she never really likes to kayak and I am more ambitious than wise.

The Mokulua Islands look closer than they are. Locals call them "the Mokes." We are Midwesterners, a different kind of hardy than the people who are home in the white sands of Oahu. My beautiful daughter, come to Hawaii for college, strong and bold since the day she was born, made this choice on an impulse, believing she could live anywhere in the world. Sandwiched between two sensitive boys, she was the baby who stayed up late and slept until nine, the two-year-old who insisted on choosing her own clothes, the ten-year-old who won the neighborhood baking contest, her cake pops more impressive than any adult creation.

So I flew four thousand, four hundred and seventy-seven miles to move Eliana into an apartment near the University of Hawaii. So far from home that I couldn't come for a quick hug or to fill her fridge. I dedicated ten August days to help her learn the names of streets, follow the route from apartment to campus, figure out how to live far from home. And when I left, we'd have only FaceTime and text to connect us. After we'd bought all the sheets and shelves that she needed, I just wanted time with her, so we drove through the green-furred mountains to the island's windward side for a day in a boat.

I don't remember any of what we said that day, just the sweet of her voice and the kiss of the turquoise waters against our tandem. It took us an hour to cross the riotous waves and reach Moko Nui, a 225-foot volcanic cone that is a government-protected haven for shearwaters. Our guide, a buff, golden twentysomething who rode the waves like she'd tamed them, called it a calm day, but I found the waves tumultuous, rising in constant aggravation. We paddled and hefted and leaned into the motion to get to the seabird sanctuary, sunlight glistening like diamonds on the water. We leaped from the boat and dragged it to the satiny beach, where a pregnant monk seal was sleeping. "Stay back." The guide waved us away, the magnificent mama's gray body gleaming in the sun.

The Hawaiian monk seal is one of the most endangered species in the world. It lives on the Mokes and, sometimes, the Johnston Atoll, 1,000 miles southwest of Hawaii. The pup will be born black and turn gray in time. Every year, these majestic creatures lose a layer of skin and fur, shedding the algae that grows on them while they forage at sea, becoming new again and again. This transformation is called the catastrophic molt, and they stay on land for the ten days or so that it takes to lose one layer and gain another.

The monk seal mama remains close to her pup for six weeks after birth, nursing and teaching the baby everything it needs to know. The mother eats nothing during that time, does nothing for herself, her child her only focus. That's all the time they get, six weeks together, and then the mother noses into the swirling ocean and swims away, leaving the young to fend for itself.

After, alone, the pup combs its birthplace for weeks, sometimes longer, learning to forage. Then, it, too, pushes off, traveling far on the journey of life, its only compass embedded in DNA.

I used to think that I would find a place that felt like home. I'd arrive and know, *this is where I belong*. I traveled far, set up apartments, unpacked my life from the boxes I'd stored it in, learned street names, yet found only loneliness in the echoes of white walls meant to welcome anyone and nourish no one. Until one day, people inhabited my definition of home. Tethered by love, by choice, by shared values and common histories.

With snorkels and masks, Eliana and I tried to see beneath the waves, but the water was murky and the masks leaked. So we left them on the beach and swam free, parallel to land. Later, we padded over dark and jagged rocks to the Queen's Bath, a tide pool roiling with minerals that turn the water emerald. It was bathy-warm, and we floated easy. The fisheries department wouldn't let us wander farther, keeping the island safe for long-winged seabirds that fly so close to the water they seem to shear off the tips of waves. That's how the shearwater earned its name. It, too, migrates far and can survive longer than fifty years. All these creatures, living by instinct, going where the wind takes them.

My daughter decided to move to Hawaii after a family trip for my fiftieth birthday. We kayaked on Kauai, hiked near blowholes on Maui, but never visited Oahu. Back home in the dark cold of a Michigan winter, she submitted an application for the university in Honolulu. The acceptance was almost immediate. I'm not sure she thought about what it would be like to move so far from anything familiar. She listened only to the call of endless sun and abundant rainbows, yearned to escape the manufactured heat of Midwest winter, shed the layers of blankets and sweaters, learn to surf the constant waves.

I understood her need to go. Once, I, too, heard the call to know the shape of this earth-home, the lilt and tenor of its different landscapes. Weeks after college graduation, I fled east and, over the course of years, set up temporary homes in New York skyscrapers and Washington, D.C. walkups. I came back when the longing for a slower pace and the friendly faces of my hometown overwhelmed my need to wander. Still, I helped her on her journey, made her new bed, folded her clothes onto shelves.

It was our last day together when we kayaked to an ocean island. And though the sun and salt had sapped every surge of energy, we eventually had to paddle back to shore. Eliana and I pulled the water and pushed it away in the shifting waves. Dip and stroke and wind-like breaths and heartbeats temple-tapping and skin buzzing in the brightness. Two-and-a-half miles felt so much farther on the return. The pad of my right arm winced, tender as a bruise. Later, it would flower purple and seethe. I'm not sure what I did to harm myself, maybe paddling too intensely, too focused on getting to home.

The surf breaks on both sides of Moku Nui. Spearfish and tiger sharks hover on the forbidden ocean side. Na

Mokulua, "two islands" in Hawaiian, older than anything human, formed more than a million years ago, is part of the Ko'olau shield, a basaltic volcano. The ancients restricted the Mokes to Kahuna, priests. Today, these tiny islands are home to twelve bird species—wedge-tailed shearwaters, red-footed bobbys, even the Great Frigatebird, a black beauty with a seven-foot wingspan.

From November to May, whales migrate past. My daughter stayed just one semester. A week after we arrived, her first boyfriend broke her heart over the phone, and she called at three in the morning in need of a mother's voice. But I think she knew she would leave even before she arrived. Going far away can help you see the beauty of home, the power of deep love from people who know you. Pulled to leave, inspired to return, each generation learns the same lesson, in its own time.

This essay was first published in MIDSTORY MAGA-ZINE on October 3, 2024. https://midstory.substack.com/p /before-i-leave-you

FINDING MY VOICE

21

— · —

TIME TO MAKE THE DONUTS

I met Cory at a B'nai B'rith dance in a high school gym when I was fourteen. I was wearing a Playboy bunny costume made from the satin striped leotard of my last dance recital and fishnet stockings plus a white puffy tail pinned to my behind. I can't believe my parents let me out of the house like that in 1986. I also can't believe I thought it was a cute costume or an appropriate way to get guys to notice me. I was naïve and young on a cool autumn night, dancing with friends as Led Zeppelin's "Stairway to Heaven" played on and on, couples shifting in slow dances to the screaming guitar.

Cory was my first boyfriend, and for the next year, we were inseparable. He was kind, tall and thin, with golden skin and golden hair. In the summer, he wore tank tops and rode a motorcycle. My parents forbade me from riding behind him. That was likely a safety issue, and maybe safety was their greatest concern, as they tried to stop me from dating him at all because he was three years older than me. When Cory left for college that fall, they refused to pay the long-distance bill for my late-night calls to his university dorm room from the quiet of my pastel bedroom, thinking it would stop the relationship then and there. But I've always been scrappy. To pay the phone bill, I got a job at Dunkin' Donuts.

Working that first job was not just about having money of my own; it was about grasping freedom, being in the world among adults who were not my parents, feeling necessary, useful, developing competence at simple skills like cleaning, serving, managing people. Behind the counter or in the back of the bakery, I had access to a secret world, and in that world, I came alive.

I also learned the secrets behind the donuts—how to fill them, how to shape them, how to bake them, how to neatly arrange them in a cardboard box on a busy weekend morning with a line out the door and people clamoring for a clean dozen. I earned money for my long-distance calls and also the sweet taste of independence. Never mind that I needed a ride to get to and from work because I wasn't old enough to drive. When I was there, I had conversations that my parents were not privy to, learned things that expanded my world—like how to be content, how to start a weekend morning with a cup of hot coffee and a warm pastry, how to wait patiently in a long line and believe that what you receive at the end was worth your time.

But only once did they let me fill the donuts.

Three months in, my manager showed me the beige machine on the counter behind the swinging door. I dumped filling into a wide, high funnel—strawberry, raspberry, custard. At the bottom, a metal spear protruded, and that's where I'd stick a donut, push a button and shoot filling into the round, soft dough.

The settings ranged from zero to ten, and my manager said three was the magic number to shoot enough filling but not too much into a donut. But you know how it is, when you bite into a jelly donut, taste the sweet, slick ooze in two bites, maybe three, and then you're left with just pastry for your remaining bites? *Not fair!* Championing customer rights, I wanted to fill them fully, make donuts heavy with sweetness. A jelly donut should be filled with jelly, I reasoned, and I was determined to make it happen. When my manager left, I cranked the machine to seven. How satisfying, to make a decision and see it through! I would right a long-held wrong. Customers would be grateful, elated. They'd come back for more and more.

Except, whenever I grabbed one of the donuts I had filled to add to a customer's dozen, my thumb pressed in at the middle. The donuts were so heavy with filling that they sagged in my grip, each one ruined.

From then on, I poured hot chocolate into Styrofoam cups, cooked eggs in the microwave for breakfast sandwiches and spread tuna salad onto croissants. I wiped coffee stains from counters, swept and mopped, chatted with police officers who lingered. I ladled soup into bowls, counted donut holes into cartons. I took money and gave change. But I never again filled the donuts.

***

While Dunkin' was my first paycheck job, I babysat for years before I tied on the pink and orange apron and served strangers coffee. After a year at the donut shop, I worked at an aerobics studio, a coney island[1] restaurant, a dry cleaner and a food court, and I loved every one of those experiences. It was always expected that I'd go from high school to college and, from there, choose some respectable white-collar career that would have me living in the kind

---

1. Coney island restaurants are a Michigan thing, having nothing to do with Coney Island, NY. They are diners that specialize in hot dogs with chili, onions and mustard over top.

of no-need-to-worry good fortune that I'd had as a child. I never considered what I'd like to spend my days doing; what kid does? I pondered the careers deemed accept-able by my community: doctor, lawyer, businessperson. I'd been queasy when we dissected frogs in high school and I hate having blood drawn, so medicine was out. Everyone seemed intent on becoming a lawyer, but I didn't really want to spend my days arguing, even though my parents said I was good at it. So business it would be, even though what brought me the most joy was putting pen to paper, writing stories, interviewing others and recording what they had to say for wider sharing.

In college, I was a staff reporter at the *Michigan Daily*. I worked for a local publisher, writing newsletters for their clients. I freelanced for the *Ann Arbor News*. I took every creative writing, journalism and literature class I could add to my schedule. Still, I never considered turning that love of words into a career.

Until one day I realized that people get paid for what I loved to do.

I spent the first fifteen years of my adult career as a journalist in New York City, Washington, D.C., and the suburbs of Detroit. I was on staff and I was a freelancer, writing for money, my name in print over and over again. It was fun. It did not feel like work.

Cradling the phone to my ear, the buzzing static of another person at the far end of the line, I whipped out questions, probed for answers. In 1995, when I listened to the beat poet Allen Ginsberg recite his epic poem "Howl" on the steps of the U.S. Supreme Court building, I scribbled notes in a reporter's notebook until my hand hurt. He kept going for more than an hour, and I drank in every word, every roll of the tongue, every spit-flying exclamation in the white wind of an overcast day.

When I interviewed the feminist Jewish writer Adrienne Rich and attended her reading in a church on Capitol Hill, a dark wooden cross dangling over the small woman of strong stature and voice, I wove the details of the setting with the words she spoke. Years later, when I asked if I could use the notes from our interview to write another article, she said, "That story has been written. Write a new story." *Do the work.*

The poet Philip Levine wrote a whole book about *What Work Is*, and I peel back its cover often. Philip Levine came from Detroit, and he was Jewish, too. He describes lines of workers outside factories, raindrops on upturned faces waiting for shift jobs. Work that makes one sweat and breathe hard, the heart pounding in your ears.

But at some point, the money became my motivation more than the meaning, and that's when everything fell apart. I pivoted from journalism to marketing, started a company and employed contractors and part-time staff. I became a manager, which I hated and was not very good at. I just wanted to write, to play with words. So eventually, I summoned the courage to return to writing and to myself.

Last summer, on a black lake in northern Canada, it occurred to me how backwards we Americans do things. We choose a career and then build a life around our work. We escape for a few fleeting days only when given permission and believe we are cramming all the meaning of our lives into those rare vacations. It is difficult to be authentic in the busy world. Only in the quiet natural one can we hear our subtle voices, know the person at the core.

The same parents who wanted me to argue in court for my career taught me to take chances, to dream big. At twenty-seven, I went freelance, started working for myself. My mother said, "If you don't try it, you'll always wonder if you could have succeeded."

My dad was an entrepreneur himself, so he knew that dreams, desire and hard work could pay off. So, I've worked for myself since 1998. There have been difficult years and easy ones, times when I worried I'd never find another client, and times when there were so many, I worked way too many hours, day and night and weekends, to satisfy everyone but myself. The work drove me, and I felt useful.

On that Canadian lake, I spent the night on an island with no Wi-Fi, no showers, only outhouses to do our business. There were no city lights to intrude on the peace of the woods. The sun set like a yolky egg behind the trees, birch and fir and pine, streaking gold on the glassy lake. The water was so clear it was nearly quivering. All the red canoes were perched on wooden planks, upside down to dry. The grass was sprinkled with coppery pine needles.

I am trying to redefine what work is—to understand that work is something deeper, more meaningful, a drive to contribute to making the world better. That happens in many places, not just in an office or with the exchange of money.

A few years ago, I hefted a shovel into the grass behind my house and pulled out swaths of sod. I cut deep and wide, to expand the garden that I had tended and cultivated, nurtured and noticed, for years since we bought this brick house. I wanted to expand the garden simply by the work of my hands, eliminate the grass and bury seeds into rich soil, grow vegetables to feed my family. I did this in between client demands and stories that needed writing, settled into the fragrant earth, clawing my fingers into the soft soil.

It took a full week of digging and pulling, tossing and

starting over, to achieve my goal, but I did it, and now the tomatoes burst in yellows and reds at summer's end, the zucchini grow big and fat. There are problems—fungus and plant disease and pests, too much rain or not enough—but nothing I can't handle. Each year I learn more about what I am capable of. I needed to heft and toil so that I could know it was possible, to see firsthand the sweat trailing down my slick skin and feel the burn of a hot sun. I grew up believing hard work was what other people did and that a job was, by definition, an obligation and nothing fun. I've changed that perspective simply by living in the moments. Hard work can be heart-bursting, invigorating, a good and meaningful way forward.

22

— · —

WORK

My alarm rang at six. I hit the top of the clock and flopped an arm across my eyes. It was already sunny in Manhattan, a summer day starting early, beckoning me out of bed.

But I was tired, up too late waiting for Jack to call. And besides, Mikell would be waiting for me. Mikell, who was always smiling, his coffee-bean skin shining under an early sun, his muscular legs bare below his shorts. We'd worked together for a year, and I still had no idea how old he was. The rest of our co-working huddle of young journalists wondered—Derek, Seth and me, a posse of business reporters at *American Metal Market*, a daily newspaper for the metals and mining industry. Mikell remained tight-lipped, always smiling. He was older than us, calmer, more serious about the work and a good friend.

We worked in an old office building in Midtown, where the windows opened enough to smell the heat of the asphalt and feel the spit of slanting rain. I had graduated from college two months earlier, and my greatest disappointment with the work world was being cooped up under the glare of fluorescent lights for the bulk of each day, never knowing the feel of the weather. I wanted to run free on more than just the weekend.

The phone rang. "I just wanted to make sure you're up."

Mikell was calling to confirm I wouldn't blow him off like I had the week before. I grunted into the phone. He laughed. I could practically hear his smile.

"Stop smiling. It's too early," I barked then giggled.

I slid my legs over the side of the bed and stood on the parquet floor. It was 1993. I'd moved to New York City three weeks after graduation and signed a lease for a cookie-cutter apartment in a Murray Hill high-rise. I couldn't afford Greenwich Village or the Upper East Side, and it was years before I knew anything about being a religious Jew to care about living near synagogues and kosher-keeping singles on the Upper West.

Three nights earlier, my on-again, off-again boyfriend Jack had slept beside me in my narrow bed. He was like my shadow, always present but never quite there, the bad boy I couldn't let myself forget. He'd also moved to New York to work on Wall Street, and we'd meet up on city streets, side-stepping puddles and ducking under awnings to steal kisses.

The night before, I'd stayed up late reading Philip Levine's poetry collection, *What Work Is*. I counted all the types of work I'd been tasked with, my relationship with Jack topping the list.

He was five-foot-seven and skinny, with strong hands. I'd glance at his hand in mine and feel like he could hold me up just by his fingers. His eyes were the creamy brown of milk chocolate, and his voice had the deepness of a sigh in the forest.

But he was a jerk.

"I don't know what you see in him," Derek said repeatedly. Buzzing with energy, he sat across from me at work.

"I don't know what you see in Jack," he repeated when I ignored him.

My look was a plea. *Not now, not again.*

He shook his head. "I'm not going to keep quiet. You mope around the office every time he doesn't call. Get over him. Forget him. Move on."

I looked at Seth, his long ponytail flat on the back of his heavy metal T-shirt. He wore skinny jeans before they were a thing and slunk around the office, taking the verbal beatings of our redheaded editor, leaving precisely at five to make love to his girlfriend. When Derek got honest, Seth avoided my gaze. I sought refuge in Mikell's eyes, but he stuffed a piece of sushi into his mouth and looked away. They were good friends, and I needed them more than I knew.

Every few weeks, the four of us headed for half-price sushi at Makko. The place was large for Manhattan, extending deep into the bowels of a nondescript building near Korea Town. It was lit by shaded bulbs that swung over booths. We stuffed our coats in corners, ordered rolls and sashimi, salads and miso soup and Japanese beer.

"You guys suck," I said, dousing my California roll in too much soy sauce. "Who asked you? Are any of you in a relationship? Well, except Seth. Seth, don't answer." I smiled in his direction. He shot a weak smile back, furtively glancing at Derek, as if for permission to weigh in.

On Saturday morning, when I could play tennis with Mikell and forget the disappointments of my heart, I picked up the poetry book, fingering the pages. Jack's call had never come. I had dozed off late, mid-page. It wasn't the first time he hadn't called when he promised to.

Jack and I had met on the first day of junior year and dated for the rest of college, breaking up and reuniting several times. Why couldn't I let him go? Derek's question was a good one.

The Saturday morning sunlight was already bright. Mikell and I had planned to play at seven, sharp. I'd be late if I didn't hurry, but I leafed through the dog-eared pages, scanning memorable lines: *No one takes my hand and leads me to bed/ to mouth agonies of darkness/When this passes/how will I know I was ... alive*[1].

I put it down on the bed, grabbed my racquet and headed out.

---

1. excerpt from Philip Levine's poem, "Burned"

23

—·—

SHORT SKIRTS AND SCRUNCHY SOCKS

By the time I quit working at Woody's, a three-story bar in a hip suburb, I'd memorized a list of twenty-three beers on tap. When someone ordered a Black & Tan, I watched the bartender pour a half glass of Bass Ale then hold a bent spoon above the froth and tip the Guinness tap to ninety degrees. A long, brown drool, viscous and thick, settled onto the bowl of the spoon, and the separation remained in the glass. It was pretty cool to look at. Black & Tan is to be sipped and savored, but my customers chugged so they could order another before I walked away. That was what we hoped for—more orders meant more tips. But as I watched their long necks taking in the thick liquid, looking so much like my East Coast ex in his late-night-drinking fervor, I thought we all must live some sort of lie.

I became a waitress because I was lonely. Twenty-seven and single, living in a post-war bungalow that I owned on the outskirts of Detroit, I worked long days as a freelance journalist and part-time adjunct college professor, typing on the computer in my loft office at a desk that faced a wall. Double-hung windows gave glimpses of my neighbor's upstairs room and a sliver of sky. I left my desk to retrieve the mail, wave to neighbors on porches, in yards, or as they parked their cars parallel to the curb, but most of the time I was alone in an empty house whose old plank floors echoed under my bare feet.

I slept in a bedroom on the first floor, with crystal antique knobs on the doors. A cordless phone sat on the nightstand. I parked my car in the double garage at the back of the driveway. When I got home late, I crept to the side door, random reports of rape and murder (not necessarily in my neighborhood) vivid in my head. But I was never assaulted, never shoved inside my house by a masked intruder or pulled into a moving car by men with evil grins. I don't know what I was afraid of, other than my own shadow.

When the loneliness got too loud, I filled out an application at Woody's. My only waitressing experience had been a summer in college at a coney island restaurant, where I wore a burgundy polyester dress, white socks and Keds and blended Oreo milkshakes for my brother and his friends. There, I balanced small white plates on my open palms two at a time, delivering hot dogs smothered in chili, onions and mustard to tables of men in white shirts and ties out of their offices for a quick, cheap lunch.

At Woody's, I'd have to balance open bottles and mixed drinks on a tray above my head as I bumped through late-night crowds of drunks. It was an odd choice of work, since I'd been trying to become a religious Jew for three years, thinking a community could erase my loneliness by finding me a husband and giving me a purpose. Now, I was applying to work at the most non-kosher of restaurants. Religion drew me because no one I dated in secular circles was eager for marriage, and I was. In fact, the minute I brought it up, any guy I was dating stopped returning my calls. I met men who were fine to grind in bed late into the night or see movies with, but commitment wasn't on their minds or in their hearts. At least not to me.

At Woody's, I'd have to work Friday nights, when religious Jews observed the Sabbath. My religious friends did not drive, work or handle money from sundown Friday until Saturday night, living according to the laws of the Torah. I took the job knowing I'd serve clam chowder and cheeseburgers and count change for twenties on the night when I wished to be lighting candles and falling asleep to a cacophony of crickets and bullfrogs.

But the religious path wasn't taking me to my desired

destination fast enough, so I traded modest long skirts and thick tights for short skirts and scrunchy socks. I tied an apron around my waist and learned to combine half-filled bottles of ketchup after my shift ended. I made an effort to look and act like my colleagues, who moved like the breeze, but it didn't come easily to me; I elbowed and jostled and spilled drinks trying to learn how to balance and run at the same time.

On breaks, I slurped the very soup my religious mentors would never dare to taste. It was warm and soft with a bite of pepper. I sank my teeth into Monte Cristo sandwiches, ham and cheese grilled to greasy, lapped up potato skins oozing with bacon and cheese and sour cream. I knew God wouldn't strike me down for eating *treif*. I'd grown up secular, believing religious transgressions and their imagined punishments were manmade. My interest in religion was fully about finding a place to belong and a person to love me forever.

I kept a little red notebook in my back pocket for orders, taken from the stack I used for researching articles during the day. Everyone else memorized customers' orders, even five tables in a row, and they were rewarded with much-higher tips. I kept a cheat sheet of specials on the first page of my notepad, wrote in my own shorthand, *chix strips* and *greek-no cheese*. Though I tried, I feared I would never measure up—in the bustling restaurant or in the community I yearned to be part of.

Everyone at Woody's complained about money. "When you worry about money, you're really worrying about being loved," my therapist had said. I didn't admit my worries aloud, but I listened to theirs, glad to be in their company, where I didn't have to have it all together.

Every night, whispers ran through the crowd of workers: *The owner's coming tonight; look busy.* We wiped down new menus that hadn't had time to turn sticky from spilled beer or hot cheese. *Look busy.* One server ran around, telling everyone behind her hand, *He's in a blue blazer, watch for him.* But the boss never came, not once when I worked there, even as we worried in corners, praying not to be fired or drop a bottle in front of the mythic Big Man. I may have been the worst server in the place, and while I did not see that job as a career move or even a role I cared much about, I didn't want to be fired. In more than a decade of working, I'd never been let go from any employment, and my weak ego could not withstand yet another rejection.

The work was draining, the customers fascinating—kind people smiling into their straws. I found stories in the crowds, though I never had time to write them. I was convinced my first novel would come from the tales of my patrons, who in my imagination became "Cheers"-like regulars who knew my name. I imagined laughter-filled after-hours with rippled bartenders sharing revelations as freely as hugs.

Sometimes, I ducked into the kitchen for a few minutes away from the pressure of placing orders fast and praying for them to come quickly. The shooting spray of the dishwasher was like a baptism; droplets gleamed off just-cleaned silverware. Everything was fast—the motions, the turnover, the drinks, the people. I stopped judging frat-boy customers who asked for my pen to take down a girl's phone number. Every request was a momentary respite, a chance to breathe, to process the fast-moving moments of my shift, to notice and listen and ponder.

When work was slow, I eavesdropped on customers' conversations—pondering a couple at table 210, who took separate vacations, or the pretty boys at 240, with earrings, reflector sunglasses on their foreheads, skin-tight T-shirts and corduroys to the knees. The guys at 231 played darts and ordered kamikazes, slipping me a twenty-dollar bill to cover the girls at the next table.

I spent most of my time on the second floor, pulling open the wide windows. Once, I served customers on the roof. As night fell in curtains, customers made a pilgrimage up two winding staircases until they stood under the sky. Like a cruise ship, the railings were high enough to prevent people from falling, the breeze swirling around a buzzing crowd. I worked the roof on my last night of training, elbowed my way through the sweaty crowd, my shins knocking into tables, my tray teetering. I spilled drinks as customers told me they'd already gotten theirs from someone *faster*.

Other servers working the roof that night were shorter than most of the customers but had no trouble one-handing trays above their heads. The roof was full of cornices and hideaways, but the drinkers stayed in the center or hovered around the bar. Orders went in at one end, and drinks in plastic cups came out the other; it took me so long to elbow my way through the crowd to pick up my orders, and I was never fast enough. "Sucks for you to lose my money," one guy said as he sipped his beer.

My life by day was starkly different from the one I lived at night. At home, I wrote to the sound of car doors slamming, phones ringing and lawnmowers humming. Working at the bar, I didn't have time to think. It may not have introduced me to new best friends, but at least the pace was so fast I could lose the loneliness for a while. I came home after streetlights had flickered off; if I squinted, I could almost see the contours of constellations. My neighbor who slept with his window open had already turned down his TV, but I could still see the white static in his window.

The summer wore on, becoming sticky and airless. I got home so late, but I couldn't fall asleep. After last call but before closing one night, I talked with a bartender with a golden goatee.

"I never sleep after work either," he said. "I open a beer and sit on my porch."

I've always had a hard time falling asleep. When I worked until two, I was wound up until the sun rose. So I was in no rush to get home after closing. I slid into a vinyl booth and kicked back shots with my co-workers. I sat beside super-thin waitresses and their butch-protector friends, bigger women who had worked there longest and stood guard over the too-cuties; once, they invited me to join them for breakfast at Denny's. It was four a.m., and while I wanted friends, I didn't go. What if I didn't fit in? I drove home to Alison Krauss on the radio and the low rumble of my older boyfriend's sleepy voice over the phone in New York.

Late at night, the darkness has a light to it. I poured a glass of pink wine and peeled off my socks, put a saucepan to boil half-filled with water and pulled a box of macaroni and cheese from the cupboard. As the clock ticked toward morning, I slid back the shower door, stepped under the pelting water and threaded apple-scented shampoo through my hair to erase the smoke from the bar that had coated my curls.

After, I pulled on a sweatshirt and padded out to the backyard with a full bowl and a fork and sank into a deck chair under the waning moon. The night was at its blackest before the dawn. I wasn't the least bit scared.

That job taught me that I loved being up when the world was asleep. I found a new kind of confidence in the dawn that had eluded me.

But I could not abandon my desire to become religious. The tight pink T-shirt with the restaurant logo and old jeans were so far from the uniform of an observant Jew. I inhabited a different world from my peers at Woody's, but I also lived differently than the Orthodox community I wanted to join. I lived in a world of my own creation, and I wasn't yet confident enough to be okay with that.

"Maybe we'll come one night for a drink to see you at work," said Yael, a rabbi's wife with five kids and a silky voice, who had taken me under her wing on my quest to become religious. She was so accepting, but I hoped she and her MBA-rabbi-husband would never visit me at Woody's. I was embarrassed by the short skirt, tight shirts and desperation that propelled me into that job. It was no wonder I couldn't connect with co-workers. Straddling worlds is no way to fit in anywhere.

Suzanne, the dark-haired server who trained me, had

a two-year-old daughter named Sunshine. She ordered salads because they were free to employees and grilled cheese sandwiches from the kiddie menu for her daughter. Clutching a Barbie, the little girl slid back and forth in a booth.

"She keeps like ten Barbies in the bathtub," Suzanne said as she shoved lettuce into her mouth. The little girl's hair kept falling into her eyes. "My friend Tony stayed at my house last week, and he took a shower and stared at all those dolls and said he'd never showered with so many women at once."

A third of the waitresses were single mothers—some divorced, some never married, all raising children on $2.62 an hour plus tips. A few were paying for college, and the rest were working until they decided on a career path. Everyone professed to hate the job, but no one quit except for me.

I only worked at Woody's for one month. By then, marketing reps and editors were calling with work that paid more in one hour than ten at the restaurant.

"I'll be back to work after my trip," I promised the cute manager who'd given me the job. His wife had been a student in the English class I'd taught at Wayne State University the previous winter. By then I was dating Chris, my former editor. We'd spend July driving west in his little brown car, through plains and cornfields. We'd never make it to the Rockies, hiking in northern Wyoming and visiting an Indian battlefield in southern Montana before turning back toward home. Our relationship was like movie love. We slept on white sheets in bed-and-breakfasts, swiping thick hunks of toast through runny yolks in the morning, all smiles over a shared newspaper.

Quitting Woody's cemented my sense of failure. Could I ever work with my hands and do it well? Would I ever blend into a community, be welcomed as one of the crowd?

When I walked into Woody's on warm afternoons, the leaves looked golden in the sun. I thought I could hear poetry writing itself in my head. On my last Thursday there, a city council candidate hosted a happy hour for campaign volunteers. He occupied four long tables against the wall; the next five were reserved for a bachelorette party. A corporate group gathered near the pool tables and low-hanging lamps.

"We're expecting more people," said a guy in a kelly green tie, his eyes begging for stools, though I didn't have any to give him. "Can we set up an appetizer table? It's on the company."

Four of us pooled our tips because no one could handle a whole party alone. It was my favorite kind of work—sharing the pressure in the company of others. I could be introverted and still take home a lump of cash, probably more than if I had worked alone. We had each other's backs. We could be a team, for a time.

As evening graduated into night, the wind blew clammy through open windows. A storm was coming. I clutched stacks of napkins and whisked glasses off full tables, filling the space with sloshy pitchers. At eleven, a manager let one of us go. The remaining four of us huddled by the coffee pots, counting tips, divvying up money. I was second to leave.

I'd hoped my last night would be slow so I could leave early, but business was steady, and the clock clicked past one. Blue-suited twentysomethings lingered late, their gazes begging *just bring our drinks*, as if they could assume all sorts of things about me because I worked there, while they wore white collars and spent long days in corner offices. *If they only knew*, I thought. After I dropped off their drinks, I debated with my co-workers whether Ireland was a developing country.

My romance with Chris ended in August when he poured chicken broth into a teacup I'd reserved for dairy foods as I tried to keep kosher.

"Don't you know what's important to me?" I spat.

"Do you think I did it on purpose?" he asked softly.

Ten years later, Woody's was still throbbing with patrons, but I was never one of them. I couldn't go back. My
time there had been an island. I'd married, had children,
and divorced by then, and I no longer minded the loneliness. As a mother of three, I relished time alone, cherished
the quiet of contemplation. My desk still faced away from
the window, even though I lived in a bigger house with a
yard that bloomed bright green all summer long and where
the best sounds were the cries of glee from my children
pumping their legs on swings and running in the grass.

I'm sure the sun shone on that loft office in my solitary
bungalow, but I never saw it. In the new house, in my
growing family, it was what I looked for. On a clear day,
I smiled at the light cascading in long, mellow streams.

24

— . —

HONORING THE DEPARTED

I knelt at my grandfather's grave, ran my fingers over the letters of his gray stone.

"Hi, Grandpa," I said. "This is Asher—he's named for you. I miss you so much."

"Read me all the words, Mommy," Asher said.

I pointed to Hebrew letters then English ones.

"*Alef, shin, resh*. That's your name." I pulled him close, my face in his soft curls.

Grandpa had been gone five years, and this was his *yahrtzeit*, the anniversary of his death on the Hebrew calendar. October, turning from summer to fall with golden leaves and cool breezes. Grandpa's grave was so close to the cemetery road that I'd left my five-month-old, Shaya, in the car with my daughter, Eliana, who was turning three that week and afraid of stepping near graves. The door and windows were open to the breeze.

While the Jewish obligation for remembering the departed falls on the children, not the grandchildren, I'd come often to my grandfather's grave. Even though I knew he was not in that soft ground, kneeling beside the stone and saying a prayer made me feel like I was with him.

In his second year of preschool, Asher asked constant questions: "Where do people go when they die, Mommy?" and "Does it hurt to die?"

I was a religious Jew at the time, so I said people go to live with God above the clouds when they've finished all the good work they have to do on Earth.

"Usually, it's when they're very, very old," I said.

I ran my fingers over the cool stone. Grandpa's skin had been glass-smooth, his laugh long and throaty, his hands big and soft. He met my grandmother through the mail during World War II, when he was stationed in Brazil. They wrote letters for a year and married two weeks after they met in person, after the end of the war. He came to Michigan because his father, an Orthodox immigrant from Poland, believed women should live near family.

Grandpa's life in Michigan wasn't easy. He never quite escaped the shadow of his mythic father-in-law, Grandpa Louie, the man I'm named for. When Grandpa Louie died, the Detroit city council cleared a two-block radius of snow from around my grandparents' house so the funeral procession could get through.

Asher walked among the headstones. Grandpa is buried in the same row as Grandpa Louie, alongside my grandmother's family, under a large stone marker bearing her family name: Woolman. I have no idea where Grandpa's parents and eight siblings lay in eternal rest. But the location of the dead is more for the proximity of the living anyway.

Grandpa Louie ran a meat-packing plant in Detroit's Eastern Market, and all the workers called him uncle. His legend looms so large in our family that I know next to nothing about his wife, Great-Grandma Evelyn, who's buried beside him.

Beyond her stone is my grandmother's sister, Auntie Barbara. She had a smoker's voice and a warm smile. At her suburban ranch house, the scent of cigarettes had seeped into the furniture. Auntie Barbara died young. My parents did not take me to that funeral.

The first funeral I attended was for Jason, a boy two grades older than me, who lived four houses down with a pool in the backyard where we swam in summer. At eleven, Jason was crushed by a pool table that had been propped against a wall in synagogue. When it started to slip during Hebrew school, he and a friend tried to prop it up. (Why was a pool table propped against a wall in the first place?)

It was a gray March afternoon when a neighbor knocked at our door and pulled my father onto the porch. They walked down the street, my father's hands behind his back, his head bowed. When he returned, he pulled my mother into a room and closed the door. The next day, I wore my best skirt to a filled funeral home, where adults wailed and wept.

When they went to the cemetery to bury the small coffin in the hard ground and throw fistfuls of dirt onto it, my next-door neighbors took me to lunch. But they let me attend *shiva*, and I wanted to do something to comfort his parents. Writing has always been the way I make sense of the world and share my deepest, most profound feelings, so I made a memorial newsletter to give to them.

Every room of their house was packed with people. Trays of brownies and cookies sat on the coffee table, deli trays in the kitchen. People milled around, murmuring things like *he was so young, too young to die, such a shame.*

In my teens, two of my classmates died. A boy named Matt played his first two minutes on the high school basketball court then collapsed in the locker room of heart failure. The next day, we walked around like zombies, counselors encouraging us to talk about our feelings.

Brad died freshman year of college. An epileptic, he suffered a grand mal seizure in his dorm room alone. I drove home for the funeral and couldn't wait for it to end so I could return to the freedom of school and the belief that I'd live forever.

I was afraid of death for a long time, perhaps because of the permanence of it and the inexplicability of what comes next, what all of this hard-earned time alive means, only to have it end so abruptly and finally. But when my father was dying, he was calm while the rest of us fretted. "There's nothing I can do about it," he reasoned. "Why get upset?"

I'm never alone in the cemetery. Past the gates, I breathe in the quiet, peaceful air. It is a place of comfort, not fear. The stones tell stories, of lives well-lived, of courageous people, of characters and legacies and love.

There, it's easy to remember the people I've loved and lost. Like my grandfather standing proud and rushing through a mumble of Friday night prayers, the wine-full kiddush cup in his hand shaking with the words. Or the way his eyes welled up at meaningful moments. Or how he giggled with my grandmother during our Sunday phone calls, each of them on separate phones when landlines were a thing.

My grandfather died in the middle of the Jewish harvest holiday of Sukkot, known as *z'man simchatenu*, the time of our joy, a time when we are not supposed to mourn.

When Grandpa died, I couldn't set aside my grief. I was

five months pregnant with Asher, and though I needed closure, I let religious friends persuade me not to go to the cemetery, out of superstition that a pregnant woman should not walk among the dead.

I attended the funeral, sat shiva at my parents' house, then returned to my religious world for a raucous holiday dinner at a long table filled with young couples and the river-rush of conversation. Though I wasn't hungry, courses kept coming—sweet spareribs, squash kugel, rice with mushrooms, chicken, meatballs, salad. A baby slept in a stroller; married women wore ink-sleek wigs to cover their hair as our religion dictated. I tucked all my hair up in a hat, covering enough to fit in.

ThoughI am not religious anymore, I still love Sukkot. We eat meals in a hut on the grass, gazing up through evergreen branches to the stars above. I think of my grandfather who died during this holiday of redemption, who rests eternally under a grove of trees, in a quiet and soft ground fragrant with the scent of living things. I believe we are connected before, during and after life to all the elements. After his funeral, I wish I had gone to the cemetery, been allowed to wail and feel the fullness of my loss. I wish I'd had the courage to make up my own mind, to not be swayed by those I thought knew better than I.

So now I go, and it brings me a new kind of peace. After

visiting Grandpa's grave, I drove the car down another path and pulled Shaya from his baby seat.

"You can't stay in the car, Eliana," I said. "We have to walk too far; I won't be able to see you." She reluctantly stepped onto the grass. Asher bounded ahead, skipping between stones.

"Look, Grandpa Sid's Hebrew name was Shaya, see?" I pointed when we got to the family stones on my father's side, his parents and paternal grandparents. "You are leaving a legacy," I whispered, as if they didn't know, and patted the head of the baby who bore my other grandfather's name.

Asher darted between gravestones.

"Ashi!" yelled Eliana. "Don't go too far. I don't want you to die!" Her blue eyes went wide, her mouth in an O.

I took a breath and closed my eyes. It was hard to teach them about the mysteries of life. These visits reconnected me to people who made my life possible. Soon, I would pile my children into the minivan and amble out of the quiet cemetery, joining fast traffic on gray streets. That was the way of our life most days. *Rush rush rush, go go go.* I wanted to keep a piece of the quiet with me, but even as I drove away, opening windows for a last clean breath, Asher was calling out and pointing to things we passed, having already forgotten the sanctuary of the trees. A train passed, screaming its whistle.

"Look, a train!" he shouted. It was a blur under blinding sun.

I put on my blinker and searched for a break in the traffic.

25

—·—

WAITING FOR MY FATHER TO DIE

I'm going to miss you so much. I choked out the words as I stroked his hand, my thumb grazing the smooth outline of his fingers, the soft pad of his palm.

I'm going to miss all of you, he said. Outside, the world was white and swirling, cold and hollow. My father lay on a hospital bed in the den in my childhood home.

I cried a lot during the two years of my father's illness. I cried when the doctor gave thirty percent odds of survival with his diagnosis of acute myeloid leukemia, an incurable blood cancer, and again two years later when another doctor said there was nothing more to do. I cried suddenly and unexpectedly—while driving my children to sports or school, in meetings with clients, during every episode of *This Is Us*.

Before he got sick, I had believed that my parents would live a very long time, that we would be the exceptional family—no sudden heart attacks or prolonged illness. They'd live into their 90s, maybe beyond 100, and we'd celebrate every birthday and laugh in the face of death. I assumed they'd walk down the aisle at the weddings of my four children, cradle great-grandchildren in their arms.

Dad and I were close. Three weeks after college graduation, he drove me to New York and helped me find an apartment for my first newspaper job. When my editor transferred me to the Capitol Hill bureau, Dad helped me buy furniture, took me for a fancy dinner and helped return an empty keg after a party. When I decided to move back to Detroit, he flew to Washington, D.C., packed up my apartment, and drove home with me, getting as giddy as I did when we crossed the Mason-Dixon Line.

Years later, when I started a marketing business, I celebrated with him when I landed a new client and sought his advice when I worried about not earning enough money. I vented to him whenever I had an argument with one of my teenagers or felt frustrated by my ex-husband. When I was divorcing, Dad sat in the courtroom for support as I stood before the judge, heart racing, hands shaking.

He always said the right thing, and he said it simply: *Don't worry, Lynnie. It'll all work out.*

He died at 81 and a half, a decent old age. He had perfect vision and played hockey until he was 70 in an over-30 league because the over-40s were too slow for him. He liked vodka on the rocks and a thick steak. He loved traveling to Japan, riding the bullet train and eating *shabu shabu*, and he loved his work in scrap metal. He never worried, not even when he got his diagnosis at 79, and my mother, sister and I twisted our hands and asked, *Why him?*

"Does it matter?" Dad said. "There isn't anything we can do about it."

I pored over medical explanations, desperate for answers. It was a rare disease caused by previous cancer treatments (which Dad never had), smoking (which Dad never did) or exposure to radiation or dangerous chemicals (it's possible, I guess). I could make no sense of this malady having afflicted my healthy father, and therefore I could not accept it.

I don't know if he was afraid to die. I never asked, and he never said, but that was typical. Dad focused on here and now, not on what might happen tomorrow.

Still, he fought to grab more time. Shortly after the diagnosis, Dad checked into the hospital to receive blood transfusions and to surgically insert a port for ongoing infusions of medicine to help his body produce more blood. I insisted on staying with him. I couldn't sleep on the pull-out chair, even with the sheet and pillow a nurse laid out for me. My thoughts swirled: How much time would we have? How much of it would be spent in the echoing halls of hospitals?

But my father could always sleep through anything, and while I lay awake, I watched him in the arc of moonlight coming through the window, seeing not an ashen, sick man, but the easygoing, take-it-all-in-stride father who had always been there for me.

For the next two years, my mother, sister and I accompanied Dad every fourth week to the cancer center for infusions of medicine to boost his body's ability to generate new blood, joking with nurses, propping pillows behind Dad's head, sipping coffee and scrolling on our phones to pass the time. When Dad turned 80, we flew to Utah where my brother was building a house and celebrated what we saw as a bonus birthday. I asked each of the ten grandchildren to write a message to Papa and created a book with their words and pictures. That spring, I had launched a podcast with Dad as my first guest; that episode aired on his 80th birthday, and we listened to it on vacation, tears trailing down our cheeks.

We filled the two years of his illness with conversation, laughter and meals around my parents' dining room table. Except for sleeping twelve hours a night and walking a bit more slowly, he didn't seem to decline that much, so I could lull myself into believing that we'd have more time than the doctors predicted. We even continued our years-long tradition of a weekly lunch, just the two of us—except when his blood count was too low to risk going to crowded restaurants.

After the diagnosis, my oldest son, Asher, started calling Dad regularly and the two grew incredibly close. It was like the illness supercharged their relationship.

I knew the end would come; I just hoped it would be far in the future. I wanted Dad to defy the prognosis—he'd always been exceptional.

In the middle of December, two years and some months after his diagnosis, on a dark winter night, Dad, Mom and I sat in the hospital room and waited for the doctor to update us on whether the treatments were successful. At that point, he had spent four months in the hospital, in an antiseptic room away from everyone he loved, trying one last experimental course of treatments.

The doctor's shoulders sloped, and he wouldn't meet our eyes.

"The treatments just aren't working," he said.

I felt like I couldn't breathe. Mom looked out the window. Dad seemed calm as ever.

"So what does this mean?" I asked.

"You could have two weeks or two months," the doctor said.

"I'd like a steak at Eddie Merlot's," Dad said.

"Is that okay?" I asked the doctor.

"If you feel up to it, do whatever you want," he said.

I reached for a tissue. "Saturday night," I said. "I'll make the reservation."

My aunt and uncle in Florida booked plane tickets. My aunt and uncle in town cleared their weekend calendar. We sat at the longest table in the restaurant, seven of the grandchildren crowded around one end. Dad drank orange juice, while the rest of us ordered wine and cocktails. No one toasted, "L'chaim," Hebrew for "to life." We toasted my dad and the fact that we were all there together one last time.

Ten days later, he fell. We rushed him to the hospital, where we learned that his blood count was the lowest it had ever been.

But Dad rallied. He insisted on transfusions—three units of blood, the most he'd ever had in one sitting. I didn't understand why he bothered. Early in his illness, a transfusion gave Dad energy for weeks. By the end, it gave him hours. I tried to talk him out of it.

"Why bother?" I said. "It's so hard on you, and it doesn't last long anymore. Why put yourself through it?"

Looking back, I realize he needed a burst of energy—it was time to put everything in order.

When my mother, sister and I kissed him goodbye at

the hospital that day, I thought it would be my last time touching his soft cheek. I drove home in a cloud of tears and barely slept that night, dreading the call.

But morning dawned in silence, and I decided to comfort myself with breakfast at a fancy restaurant. I sat beside a fireplace with my journal and a book. I sipped coffee, ate a Belgian waffle with berries and whipped cream. I tried to write, but nothing came. I tried to read but scanned the same page over and over.

Suddenly, my phone buzzed. A picture of my father lit up the screen.

"Lynnie." My father's voice, stronger than it had been in weeks. "Come to the hospital. I have some things for you to do."

I tore out of the restaurant. Sitting up in bed, Dad was all business. He told me where to find a folder for my parents' cars, how to return his car after he died, and who to call at the dealer when Mom's lease ended. "Make sure she pays cash for a new car," he said.

He told me to write his obituary and submit it to trade newspapers in his industry—*American Metal Market*, the Institute of Scrap Recycling Industries, and *Metal Bulletin*, along with the *Detroit Jewish News* and the *Detroit Free Press*.

"Find my resume," he said. "I was the chapter president

for the Michigan Scrap Institute. Call Tommy and Abe for quotes." He gave me their numbers.

He asked me to call his cousin and my aunt, his sister, to let them know he had days, maybe hours. He told me where to find the insurance information, what Medicare would pay for. He asked me to get his razor and have my husband come to the hospital to give him a shave.

"Tell Ashi when he goes up to get his diploma, I'm there with him," he said. I pictured my son graduating from high school six months later, a row of family members cheering as he walked across the stage, one seat empty.

I took notes on my phone, riveted to Dad's words. I would do everything he asked and do it well.

He asked me to distribute his books, to give my brother his collection of *National Geographics*, to give my daughter his 1950s milkshake maker. He asked for her to make him one last vanilla shake when he returned home later that day.

"Make sure Mom makes the right decisions," he said.

"About what?"

"Anything and everything," he said. "Hover around her."

Later that day, Dad came home by ambulance and settled into a hospital bed in the den of my childhood home, the home he built with my mother when I was a year old.

My mother had hired a team of caregivers to sit by his side around the clock. He hung on until my brother arrived from Illinois, and then he slipped into the space between this world and the next.

I kept thinking about how he'd said he'd miss us all. I wondered where he would go, if there was missing there. I believe in the supernatural, but my father, a pragmatist, always scoffed at my spiritual musings, my Runes and incense, the signs I insisted I saw in the clouds—angel wings or a heart. Days earlier, when the rabbi visited, my father had said, "When I'm dead, I'm in the ground, and that's that."

For forty-eight hours, we milled about the house while Dad passed on. This was the first time I had ever witnessed the dying process; I was surprised by how long it took.

Is he in pain? I asked the hospice nurse.

We've given him morphine, she said. *He isn't feeling anything.*

So why did it take so long to go? I was finally ready for what would come next, done with being suspended between what I knew and what I feared.

Finally, on Thursday night, a caregiver opened the den door and called for my mother.

"He's gone," she said quietly.

Mom called my siblings and me to her room, pulling us

into a huddle, our heads touching. She wailed. My sister cried. My stoic brother's face was wet.

I had no tears left. I was floating, watching everything with supreme curiosity.

Downstairs, I stared at all the stricken faces. When the funeral home representatives came to take my father's body, a young man with a scraggly beard and prayer fringes dangling over his waistband, said, "Can I see Norman?" He knew nothing about my dad except the name he'd read on a piece of paper, but with that simple question, he acknowledged my father's humanity, even in death. He saw what I saw: that my father was still a person to be cherished. I watched the man walk into the den while everyone—cousins, aunts, uncles, all ten grandchildren—fled as far from the body as they could. I wanted to bear witness, to see what happens after life leaves a person. I wanted to cling to the present, the way Dad always did.

In an hour, my father's body had shrunk, grown waxy and gray. Jews don't look upon death readily. We do not display open caskets, and we bury our kin quickly, believing the soul lingers until it is put to rest in the ground. My family always sat shiva for the shortest time possible, cut short conversations about death and never visited a cemetery unless it was for a funeral we were obligated to attend.

But I've always been different from my family. When my children were little, I took them to the cemetery where my grandparents are buried.

"There's your name," I told my youngest son, Shaya, pointing to my grandfather's grave.

I wanted to create connections between the living and the dead. I told my children stories of those I loved who had passed on. I embraced the silence of the cemetery, trodding along the soft grass, brushing my fingers over the smooth stones.

Now I wanted to look death in the face, to escort my father to the tunnel. I loved him that much.

***

In the Jewish tradition, a child is supposed to mourn the death of a parent for eleven months by reciting Kaddish, a prayer exalting the virtues of a merciful God without mentioning death or the loved one lost. Mourners recite Kaddish three times daily at services and on the Sabbath and holidays. Many people who never go to synagogue show up after a parent dies just to say this prayer. The person in mourning, or observing *yahrtzeit* (the anniversary of a death), stands while the congregation sits. The standing recite the prayer aloud, while everyone else stays silent except to say *amen*.

I had planned to say Kaddish for my father in synagogue, but because of the pandemic, I could only say it over Zoom during online services, in sweatpants in my living room. My year of mourning ended before the pandemic did, so I never got to stand amid the congregation and wait for their *amen*. I experienced the stages of loss without community, but that's probably how Dad would have wanted it. I can hear him now: *Why waste your time, Lynnie? Go do something fun. Be with the kids. Remember me with a piece of key lime pie and the Sunday* New York Times.

On the first anniversary of Dad's death, I lit the memorial candle and let it burn for twenty-four hours. The next day, I went to the cemetery with my mother and sister. Dad's name was etched on gray stone, along with his Hebrew name and his family roles: husband, father, grandfather. The dates of his birth and his death.

We laid stones on his grave as evidence that he is remembered.

"What a beautiful day," my mother said.

It was forty degrees in December with the sun shining. In Michigan, we call that warm.

In my father's last months, I saved his voicemails, but in the year and a half since he left this world, I have never played them. I hear his voice in my head, and that is enough. I miss him in the oddest moments but not constantly, as I imagined I would. I want his advice, but I don't need it. I know what he would say. More than anything, I just want to sit with him and talk...and listen. I think that never would have gotten old.

This essay first appeared in THE JEW-ISH LITERARY JOURNAL on December 23, 2021, https://jewishliteraryjournal.com/creative-non-fictio n/waiting-for-my-father-to-die-lynne-golodner/

26

ONLY LIVING BODIES BLEED

"**I** went into their bedroom and saw two beds," my niece said after babysitting for an Orthodox rabbi's children. "What's that about?"

I nodded as it all came crashing back. "Orthodox couples don't touch during the woman's period until it ends plus seven days."

Her eyes went wide.

"And they can't touch, can't pass the salt or the chicken or the baby, until the woman goes to the mikvah, the ritual bath," I explained.

"Did you do that when you were religious?"

I nodded. "But I made him sleep in the smaller bed. I kept the king for myself."

"I hope so," she said.

I learned to be a religious wife in *kallah* (bride) classes that focused on the details of a woman's body at every point in the month. It was required if I wanted an Orthodox rabbi to marry us, so I spent weeks at the kitchen table with a rabbi's wife, reading the religious laws pertaining to a woman who bleeds. She turned the pages of a pink book (of course it was pink!), read passages aloud and explained how to live the laws. As a religious wife, I would check for blood in all the crevices of my most intimate parts to confirm that my cycle had concluded.

"The vagina is like an accordion, the folds tight together until it's time to push out a baby," she said. "Then, the skin unfurls, expanding to give the child space to come forth."

In the Orthodox Jewish world, anyone with an open wound is prohibited from touching the Torah. This includes women during their cycles, even though menstruation is not a wound. The rule is not enforced for men, though they can choose to go to a mikvah at any time, and not just after bleeding—after a wet dream, for instance, or to purify before a holiday. They can go in broad daylight, with anyone noticing. They are not, like women, obligated to conceal this transformation in the darkness of late night. Women cannot go to the mikvah until after three stars shine in a night sky. Then they go quietly, humbly, into an unmarked building.

In most Orthodox synagogues, women are not allowed to touch the Torah, ever, just in case they might be bleeding. But I imagine by now, the reasons are far more vast than a simple monthly cycle, because even old women long past the age of menstruation do not have the privilege of touching or holding the holy scrolls. All the women sit behind a barrier, behind the men, told that they are holier, but relegated to being observers because they are so damn holy.

***

I came to Orthodoxy from a liberal Jewish childhood, five years after I graduated from college and after years of hooking up and yearning for a lasting relationship. I was tired of pretending I didn't want marriage and babies, and the Orthodox world is all about finding your beshert—the person you are destined to be with—and building a family. For a time, I believed following Orthodoxy's gender-defined roles would be easier than forging my way as a strong woman whom many considered "too much." And, after seeing guys run for the hills when they realized I was marriage-minded, I figured becoming religious would lead me to the wedding canopy.

Soon after I committed to Orthodox Judaism, I met my first husband. He proposed three months after our first date, and we married five months later. He was a talented musician who wore colorful clothing, and I thought we might make a creative couple. I liked that he didn't observe everything. No one does, really, even if they pretend to. He didn't care if I wore pants or sleeveless shirts or went swimming in mixed company, but some rules were non-negotiable. For instance, he never ate non-kosher food, he wouldn't tear toilet paper on Shabbat and he insisted on washing dishes on Shabbat using only cold water. He didn't object to having sex before marriage but insisted that once married, we must follow the rules strictly, separating the minute I got my period and not reconnecting until after I'd dunked in the mikvah. Since I was new to his world, I didn't have the confidence to know which laws to follow and which to ignore.

Upon the first drop of blood, we slept in two beds, could not hand each other a bowl of rice or a bottle of wine or a sleeping child. For at least twelve days every month, there was no kissing, no lingering trail of fingers. I went to sleep alone, while he stayed up in front of his computer. I cooked and cleaned; he came late to dinner. So many religious wives insisted the forced separation helped them focus on their emotional relationship, but it wasn't that way for us.

A woman begins counting "clean days" when her period ends. There must be seven before you can return to your husband's embrace. Every evening, I wrapped a white cloth around my forefinger and pushed it into my vagina to search for remnants of blood. Those cloths, sealed in white envelopes and left on the kitchen counter, found their way to a rabbi in a quiet alley who held the cloth up to the waning sunlight. He alone determined if I could keep counting. Every time, he said yes. If I spotted a speck of blood, my husband phoned the rabbi to ask if I could keep counting. It always came down to the color—bright red sent me back to day one, but any other hue allowed me to keep going. It was like they wanted us to jump through hoops, to be vulnerable to their laws, to submit entirely to hallowed rabbinic opinions, while also wanting couples to reunite quickly; sex (or rather growing families) was the glue that kept the community going.

Once I could schedule an appointment to immerse in the sacred waters, there was another round of requirements.

"Remember to scrub beneath your nails to remove any dirt," the mikvah lady instructed. "Comb out all your hair." She glanced at my hat-covered head then trailed her eyes down my body to indicate all the hair.

I stepped out of my shoes, unzipped my denim skirt, pulled my shirt over my head, stripped off my underwear. The books insisted that a woman should spend at least thirty minutes soaking and scrubbing and examining every inch to become as pristine as her wedding night. There were Q-tips and cotton balls, unscented soaps and nail clippers, emery boards and fluffy white towels to aid in the process.

To be sure, there were good things about that life. I loved taking a full day off from the busyness of the week to become quiet. On the Sabbath, we walked to synagogue, kept the TV off and lingered at the table over good conversation with interesting people. I learned to make bread from scratch. When I had a baby, meals magically arrived every day for three weeks. And when a loved one died, you would never be alone in the sadness.

But all the years that I was religious, I couldn't find the good in the forced separation around menstruation. It created distance in my marriage and resentment in me. It made me feel like my very essence, the soft and miraculous parts of my womanhood, was distasteful, to be kept at a distance.

***

I never had a relationship with my own blood. There was the pinprick test in the doctor's office, a nurse holding my finger between two of hers. A sharp poke, a searing sting of metal piercing skin, and then the coming forth of bright red. The nurse squeezed my finger to drip in a tube for testing. The blood told a story, a version of me, my body's secrets. There is no hiding from the story of the blood.

When I was seven, my mother sat on the edge of her bed, dust particles floating in the daylight from the window. She read a book aloud, with illustrations of a bee nosing into a flower, a dog climbing on another dog, a woman and a man lying on their backs in a bed, the blanket tucked under their armpits. The bee and flower led to more flowers, yellow pollen floating between them. The dogs suddenly had a litter of puppies. And after the humans lay side by side, a baby curled inside the woman.

"Do you have any questions?" my mother asked.

I was ten when I first learned about periods and their connection to baby-making, through animated movies in my fifth-grade classroom overlooking a field of dandelions. Teachers separated girls and boys. A Disney cartoon taught us that women bleed every month, and we shouldn't take too-hot showers when it happened. The female characters had no feet, only pinpoints.

I first bled two years later. I wiped it away with tissue, flushed, and scrubbed my hands in the white sink. Downstairs, I whispered the news to my mother. She pulled me into a hug, my heart pulsing thump-thump-thump. She handed me a box of pads.

"Pull off the paper and stick it to your underpants," she instructed. "Fold the used one up and wrap it in toilet paper. No one should look into the trash and see blood."

I hid the box in my bathroom cupboard.

The next morning, I snuck downstairs before my father left for work and whispered the news to him.

"That's big, Lynnie!" he said, pulling me into a hug.

My period came every five weeks or so. My mother taught me to circle with permanent marker on a wall calendar the day each period started.

"Regularly irregular," she called it when it was different every time. "It's always been that way for me, too." She smiled as if we shared an important bond.

Some Jewish scholars compare women to God in our power to create life. But monthly bleeding is a nuisance. A silent something endured as a sorority of unseemliness. I assumed boys would be grossed out by the mess, and I wondered what they learned in fifth grade—boy things like masturbation, the need to shower and wear deodorant, and how you got blue balls?

In ninth grade, during three weeks with "Mike and Mack"—Mrs. Michaelson and Mrs. McElroy, two supposedly cool moms who demonstrated how to put a condom on a banana—boys and girls gathered together in the school auditorium to learn how not to get AIDS, how not to get pregnant, and about the diseases you'd catch if you slept around.

In all the years of sex education in my public schools, there was no discussion of orgasm or mutual pleasure or hormones or the rhythm of cycles. Nothing about desire. Or intimacy. Or love. No advice about knowing your body well enough to be a willing partner. Or not needing a partner at all. Nothing about how to choose whom to love, what a healthy relationship might look and feel like. And nothing about the miracle of the human body or the beauty of life-giving blood coursing through all the crevices and folds.

***

When friends see pictures of me with my hair tucked up into a big velvet hat, they say, "I can't imagine you being religious."

When I think about the me that was religious and the me after I left Orthodoxy, I look for themes, searching for a common thread to say that the real me was there all the time. What I come to is the body—my physical form. Though the belly is a bit softer, the middle thicker, my hair shorter, the surge of delicate nerves, thumping heart, searing breath, frizzy curls and, of course, the blood, all of that is one consistent person.

A religious friend once displayed a tented sign on her dining room table that said, "Thank you for not speaking *lashon hora*" (gossip). I admired the aspiration. But the reality was different from the ideal. Now I say, don't confuse Jews with Judaism. At some point, rigidity doesn't bend, it breaks.

***

The mikvah had eighteen rooms (eighteen being the Hebrew number for *chai*, life) for women to prepare for immersion. Each room had two doors—one to go into and one that opened to a back hallway that led to the place to dunk. You are not supposed to see other women while there, to keep secret the intimacies of the marital bed.

I wrapped a robe around my body, pulled my curls into a knotted towel. On the wall, buttons sparked little lights to let the mikvah lady know I was ready. She rapped quietly, and I opened the door, padding on paper shoes to follow her to the steaming tub, where I shed the robe and stood naked in the humid air.

She picked stray hairs off my skin, inspected my palms, bent to look at my feet. Brushing her fingers along my heels, she separated my toes to look for dirt. Satisfied, she waved me toward the tub.

I descended into a mix of tap water and rain from the heavens.

"Make sure you go deep enough that your hair doesn't float," she said.

I closed my eyes, blew out from my nose, bent my knees to get low. Then I burst out of the water, covered my head with a washcloth and recited the prayer:

Barukh atah Adonay Eloheynu melekh ha-olam, asher kidshanu b'mitzvotav v'tzivanu al ha-t'vilah.

Blessed are you, Eternal God, ruler of the universe, who sanctifies us through commandments and has enjoined us concerning immersion.

"Amen!" the mikvah lady proclaimed. I submerged again, and again, as she chanted "Kosher! Kosher! Kosher!"

When I emerged, she held the robe up high to block my nakedness. The heat of a long soak had softened my skin and lulled me into calm. I wanted to head home, where I could crawl into bed and sleep easy.

But after twelve days of distance, my husband wanted me. For nearly two weeks, he'd slept alone while our babies pulled at my milk-heavy breasts, curled into my lap, nestled in my bed. Not to mention all the time I spent chopping vegetables and washing plates, vacuuming, punching dough and writing articles to pay our bills, while my husband fulfilled his "obligation" as a man, to show up in synagogue and be counted. He went daily. On Saturdays, I trailed behind, pushing a double stroller, sweating under layers of covering, the neighborhood men in fur hats and flapping jackets ignoring my cheery hello. Not only women's bodies, but also our voices were *erva*, nakedness, and couldn't be heard in the company of men. I had become religious to be accepted, and yet being religious made me invisible.

Hebrew words are defined by their roots, three letters that form a core of meaning. Rabbis insist the mikvah is all about spiritual purity. But the words—*tumah*, *taharah*, impure and pure—can't translate better than "dirty and clean" in English. It's about immersing the soul, they say. I am not a linguistic scholar, so I have to trust the translations.

But it's not just words that create separations. The community keeps men and women on opposite sides of everything. If I had grown up in that world, I might have accepted all of its idiosyncrasies. I might have welcomed the passions of a man who kept his distance because I bled, knew how to be untouchable and yet desired.

Before I was Orthodox, I loved sex. Once married, I could not find the spine-tingle of anticipation, the shiver of fingers tracing my skin. I was too caught up in the rules. My husband did not excite me. Or maybe it was the lifestyle. At night, I dreamt about the men who came before, and the memories carried me for a while.

***

I left that marriage at thirty-seven, eight years after the wedding and ten years after I became religious. I left because I wanted to love with abandon. And I was tired of putting a pin in my feminist beliefs and my strong independent streak. I welcomed back the outspoken woman who was never content to accept someone else's dictates of how to live. For the first time in my life, I was confident and happy alone.

I packed my hats into plastic boxes and shortened my skirts, pulled pants and tank tops from the dark corners of my closet. I never again went to the mikvah.

Not long after, I met the man who would become my second husband, the love of my life, the person with whom I need no barrier, no separation, no distance. We would not have children together—I had my three plus his beautiful daughter. All of my children struggle with religion.

One loves the beauty of tradition and heritage and ancestry but hates the rules. The others want nothing to do with spiritual dictates or religious rules.

I am older now and have learned to see the beauty in every stage of my body. I have embraced what makes me a woman—the messiness of monthly cycles, the power to create life—in the twilight before it disappears. I wonder if there is a blessing for when my period stops for good, a final dunk in living waters, a formal farewell to show gratitude to the power that has made me a woman, the beauty of imperfection that I have lived. Perhaps I'll create one: immerse in the roiling waters of a cold ocean or a great lake, free to see the poetry in all the moments and celebrate them in a ritual of my own making.

This essay was first published in MOMENT MAGA-ZINE on May 22, 2023. https://momentmag.com/memo ir-menstruation-only-living-bodies-bleed/

27

—·—

WHAT'S IN A NAME

"You'll feel different when you start using your Hebrew name," Bayla said.

We sat on the carpet as her children played, leaning against a sagging couch shoved against a bare wall. A corner shelf displayed wedding portraits of the oldest of her nine children. As couples arrived for Shabbat lunch, warm air floated in from the screen door that kept opening and closing, fluttering the tight curls at the back of my neck. The rest of my hair was tucked into a hat as a mark of marital modesty. I was two years into life as an Orthodox Jew, twenty-nine and newly married to a lifelong religious guy, but I had just confided in Bayla that I felt as though I was posing.

She could have said any combination of reassuring words: *It's really hard to change your whole life, it's sad to let go of what you've always known, in choosing this life you are leaving behind friends and family and that must hurt.*

She could have said, *you're totally part of us, and I hope you feel that soon.*

Instead, her response told me, *keep rejecting the people who love you, who raised you; shed everything about yourself until you no longer see the person you used to be.*

For as long as I could remember, I'd dreamt of falling in love with a man with whom I could be silly, sexy and adventurous. He'd match me in intellect, possess a quick wit and consider my hypersensitivity one of my most precious qualities. And though we'd fight, we'd make up fiercely. Beyond intense love, I wanted to be a mother (at least three kids, maybe five), and the fiery relationship that produced my beautiful children would be the iron-strong foundation for a loving, close family.

But by the time I reached my mid-twenties, a string of imperfect relationships behind me, I wondered what was wrong with me if I could not attract my one true love and life partner. Everyone I knew was into hookups and casual dating, and most guys ran scared the minute they heard the word "marriage." My father always said, "People who want to get married, get married," but I didn't quite believe that included me because he also said I was too sensitive, and others in my family called me "bossy" and said I had a "big mouth." Guys were attracted to me, but none stuck around for long or showed interested in a shared future.

There was Jack, the Catholic from New Jersey whose antisemitic father accused a waiter of "Jewing" him. When he told his dad not to speak like that in front of me, I said, "He shouldn't speak like that at all."

There was David, who was sixteen when his parents split and considered any argument grounds for a breakup. That relationship lasted until our first fight.

There was Bryan, who dumped me after attending my MFA graduation and meeting my whole family.

Others flitted in and out just as quickly. So when at twenty-six, while I was living in Washington, D.C., I experienced my first Orthodox Shabbat at a colleague's home, I was intrigued. There, I discovered a community that prioritized marriage and family, which I conflated with love and belonging.

In my colleague's Modern Orthodox community, women carried the Torah around their half of the sanctuary, wore pants and short sleeves and only covered their hair during services. They were doctors and lawyers and entrepreneurs. Their husbands seemed proud of, and attracted to, their strength. The rabbi's wife was taller than him and on Simchat Torah, her blond hair bounced as she danced in circles. She didn't hide herself, and no one expected her to.

When I moved back to Michigan the next year, I

searched for a Modern Orthodox community of my own. Unable to find one, I settled on an Orthodox synagogue led by a dynamic rabbi who wore expensive suits and had earned an MBA. He and his wife, who covered her hair with a wig and had birthed five children in seven years, welcomed everyone, even Reform and Conservative rabbis, to their table. They didn't judge me for living a nonreligious life that included premarital sex, cheeseburgers and Christian ex-boyfriends. Their unconditional acceptance convinced me that Orthodox Judaism could be a home for me.

Years later, that rabbi officiated at my first wedding. By then, he and his family had moved away, and my community had drastically changed. I proposed inviting Orthodox feminists to be guest scholars at the synagogue, but threatened by the word "feminist," the young women of the congregation shot me down.

It was during that time that I met my first husband. I was twenty-eight and writing for magazines and newspapers; he was living in New York, wanting to be a musician. We went out on a blind date while he was in town for Thanksgiving. In a community where men wore white button-downs, black hats and black suits, he wore purple. He was religious but seemed free-thinking and artistic like me, so I jumped into the relationship. We moved so fast that I ignored the warning signs: at thirty, he'd never held a job for longer than nine months; it had taken him eight years to finish college; and it soon became clear that his un-tucked flannels over white T-shirts indicated not a rebel-lious grunge phase but a debilitating depression. I thought I could help him become his best self. Interestingly, I never considered looking for a relationship where we both lifted each other up. I just hoped one day we would find in each other the true love I so desperately wanted.

Once we were married, we invited couples to Friday dinners and Saturday lunches. Amid fluttering oak and maple trees and in the harshest of winters, we walked more than a mile to sway in synagogue amid swelling voices and schmooze over cookies after services. My husband of-ten led the congregation, his voice wrapping the prayers in lovely song, and those were the moments I admired him and found him attractive. I befriended Adina, a rab-bi's wife with a kosher candy business; Beth, a preschool teacher who became religious in her twenties alongside her husband, whom she'd met in college; Rivkie, an accoun-tant, who wore sweats and shed her wig when no one was home; Khaya, who made a delicious lasagna and whose philosopher-husband gazed at her with an adoration that I envied.

But at home in the bungalow I'd bought when I was

single, I watched *Friends*, while my husband hid in the basement. I went to bed alone. When we spent holidays with his family, I felt self-conscious that I didn't know the prayers well enough to sing along with my in-laws. Rather than stay up until two a.m. to finish the Passover seder, I left everyone at the table and crawled into bed with a book.

My three babies, born within four years, distracted me from my doubts about my husband and the religious community I'd chosen. Often during that time, I found myself reflecting on a trip to Dublin I'd taken at twenty-three to visit my friend Catherine, long before I became religious in Judaism. I sat in her church on Good Friday, my frizzy hair and pale skin helping me pass as Irish, taking in the poetry and candlelight of a Taize service. The church reminded me of my Reform childhood synagogue in so many ways—soothing music, thoughtful poetry, people who wanted to be there, parishioners who were friendly and welcoming and accepting. I grew up in a Judaism that encouraged innovation—they were always adding programs or changing services to match the interests of the congregation. After all, Reform Judaism was founded on the idea that we can amend ancient traditions to meet modern times. I had more in common with Catherine's Irish Catholic community than the one I later married into.

All my life, I've searched for my people, yearning to enter a room and see faces alight with smiles and a shared knowing of *this is our place*. But in my marriage and in my community, I only fit if I wore the uniform and followed the rules. I wanted to find a place where it didn't matter what I wore, just that I was there. But in fact, four years in, when I permanently uncovered my hair, my two closest friends—Adina and Beth—stopped inviting me for Shabbat meals.

***

At lunchtime in Bayla's 900-square-foot home, her family and twelve guests migrated to long, plastic-covered folding tables. Her husband, a tall rabbi with a gray beard, sang blessings over wine and bread. As we munched on challah rolls, women brought in plates of noodle kugel, bowls of thick, long-cooked *cholent* stew containing beef, potatoes and onions, and dishes of creamy coleslaw. After the meal, the men sang in Hebrew, slapping the table to keep rhythm.

I knew the words to the songs; the deep consonants of their voices shook the room. I had always loved Shabbat, sitting among a boisterous gathering of people who wanted nothing more from a Saturday than a warm lunch and hours of conversation. But in Bayla's house, my role as a religious woman was to keep silent. I missed singing with a swelling chorus of voices, like I had done at summer camp. Now, I only sang in the car when no one was listening.

***

Before my wedding, my mother-in-law begged me to take my husband's surname. *Schreiber* was German for scribe, and since I was a writer, she insisted that meant her son and I were *bashert*, destined. Never mind that I was an author of books and articles bearing my maiden name, Cohn—which signified the biblical high priests. In the Orthodox world, a Cohn was more prestigious than a Schreiber. The *Cohanim* led the community, and I was the daughter of a *cohain*. By taking my husband's name, I let go of the clan I came from, the prestige I was born into.

Names have power. They connect you to meaning, to history, to people. A recognizable name can pave your path, make it easy to enter parts of society previously closed off. For a time, because I had felt so at home in Catherine's community, I kept a list of Irish names I wanted for my future children. Before I met my husband, I fantasized about one day taking a man's name as a sign of the deep and abiding current that ran between us. A shared name would mean we were linked by more than a legal document, by a connection that strengthened us to face a harsh world. In that energy, I could be brazen and loud, speak my mind and be loved for it.

When I was growing up, most women took their husband's name—a tradition dating to the Middle Ages, when surnames became common in Europe as people began to travel and needed to distinguish themselves from one another. European last names either identified a person's father (Johnson means John's son); a land feature or location (Underhill or Atwood, for example); a nickname based on size or trait (Little, Short, Stern); or an occupation or status—Baker or Knight.

I gave in to my mother-in-law but ignored Bayla, keeping my English first name so I wouldn't disappear entirely. Of course, my English first name isn't mine, either, not exactly—parents decide what to call their children. While a surname unites a family, first names convey parents' hopes for the future and connections to the past.

In my family, names, both English and Hebrew, mark the memories of those worth honoring. My parents gave me the English names Lynne Meredith Cohn and the Hebrew names Leah Masha. They chose Lynne, an "L" name, in memory of Grandpa Louie, the patriarch on my mother's side. Grandpa Louie was a butcher in Detroit's

Eastern Market, a basketball player for B'nai Brith and
so well-known that when he died, cars lined the streets
around my grandparents' home for blocks. He wore the
two-tone patent leather shoes and fedoras of the 1950s Rat
Pack and bought my mother her first car, long and wide
with shiny hubcaps and tail wings.

When I was little, I slept at my grandparents' house
some Friday nights. We ate Shabbat dinner in their
kitchen—brisket in bubbling tomato sauce, crisp salad,
soft bakery challah, Grandma's chicken soup flavored with
fresh dill. Saturday morning, Grandpa took me to synagogue, where I'd wander into the middle of the row in
the middle of the sanctuary where he sat wrapped in his
tallit, his arm finding its way around my shoulders while
he mumbled prayers.

On holidays, Grandpa poured sweet wine through a
funnel into a sparkling crystal decanter. Grandma baked
cherry squares and double chocolate brownies. As the sun
set outside the window, the table held homemade gefilte
fish, quivering hard-boiled eggs in crystal bowls, creamy
chopped liver. I giggled with my cousins, in the embrace of
a family following rituals handed down over generations.
My names beckon these scenes, but there's a crick in my
neck from always looking back. I needed a sense of who
I could be in the present, or aim for something brighter,

bigger and entirely my own.

***

It's been so many years since I left the Orthodox world that the people I meet now wonder how I could have been that person. "You?" they ask. "You're so strong and independent. I can't see you in that quiet little role."

They can't see me with covered hair and long skirts, as the *balabusta* cooking past midnight on a Thursday to get everything ready for the Sabbath. They can't see me sitting behind the *mechitzah,* the lattice wood divider on the women's side of the synagogue, peering through to only kind of make out the action in the men's section, their swaying to and fro in prayer, their singing and back-slapping and gossiping as the rabbi called out the page number.

When I was religious, I did a photoshoot for a forthcoming book. I wore a big-brimmed black velvet hat, all of my hair tucked up inside it. The angle of the camera shows me looking down, half of my face obscured in what I thought at the time was a poetic gaze. Now, I look at that image and see a woman hiding in a role that doesn't suit her.

I don't know how I was that person, either.

When Bayla told me to drop my English name, she was

telling me to reject myself. She was saying that to fit into her world, I'd have to become a different person. I didn't realize that my invitation to her home was conditional—the opposite of why I'd joined her community in the first place. It took seven years to realize how invisible I was. To her. To my chosen community. Even to my husband.

True love doesn't require a new wardrobe, a different name or an unnatural code of conduct. Of course I didn't fit into the Orthodox world! I was hiding and silencing everything that made me Lynne. If I didn't like the person I was trying to be...why would anyone else? I see now that agonizing over my name replaced a more uncomfortable line of questioning: Who did I want to be? And could I accept who I was?

***

Eight years after becoming Lynne Schreiber, I ended my marriage and left Orthodoxy. I gave away boxes of hats, setting my hair free in the wind. I donated long skirts and long sleeves to charity and pulled on jeans and tank tops. I spent holidays hiking forested trails with my children. On Yom Kippur, we threw chunks of bread into the rapid current of a nearby river, watching our sins drift away.

About six months before I filed for divorce, I told my

mother that I was contemplating ending my marriage.

"Don't do it because you think you'll find another, better love," she said. "Do it because you'd rather be alone than remain with him."

For the first time in my life, I was happy being alone. In fact, it felt calming. For so many years, I'd yearned for love, and the absence of a partner felt like a commentary on my desirability. I no longer believed that lack of a partner meant I was unlovable. And now I knew that if I remained alone for the rest of my life, I would be okay.

A year and a half later, I met Dan, who would become my second husband. He comes from Irish and English ancestors on one side and Jewish stock from the Black Sea on the other, and his names reveal the mix of identities he was born into. He didn't care if I took his surname, but it felt odd to keep my first husband's name, even though it linked me to my children.

I considered reclaiming Cohn, but that felt like sliding backward. I imagined dropping surnames altogether and calling myself Lynne Meredith. Or choosing something totally new, pulling from that list of Irish names I'd collected years earlier. But any change would require rigorous form-filing and office-calling, and for what?

As we packed up the house I'd shared with my first husband to move to a new home for our blended family,

I ran my fingers over my books. My first poetry collection, *Driving Off the Horizon* by Lynne Meredith Cohn; my nonfiction tome about Jewish hair-covering, *Hide and Seek,* and my second poetry collection, *Living Inside,* by Lynne Meredith Schreiber. My next book, *The Flavors of Faith: Holy Breads,* would bear the name Lynne Golodner (there wasn't room on the cover for Meredith).

In my new life, bolstered by self-love as well as the unconditional love of my children and new husband, I stopped caring about my name. Today, I answer to whatever, even when my kids' friends mistakenly call me Mrs. Schreiber. I took Dan's surname because it felt easiest. Anti-climactic, I know. But we always go to bed together, and when we align on parenting decisions or say the same words at the same time, I smile at the synergy. Dan chants, "Team Golodner!" and I pump my fist. He loves me for my strong personality, my independent streak and my no-nonsense tendencies to call-it-like-it-is. He loves my passion, too.

And finally, I love all these things about myself.

This essay first appeared in VALIANT SCRIBE on March 6, 2023, https://www.valiantscribe.com/post/what -s-in-a-name-non-fiction-essay-by-lynne-golodner

28

— · —

VOICE

"*A fall of voice, regretted like the nightingale's last note.*" ~ *William Wordsworth*

I try to speak, and my voice catches, an acorn lodged in my throat. Well-meaning friends say: *Maybe it's not something to power through. Study the throat chakra. What is the silence trying to tell you? Are you listening?*

***

Just using my voice makes it harder to use my voice. The voice therapist, Juliana, says a polyp on the vocal cords rarely resolves through therapy, but because mine is small, we can try.

She tells me to blow through a straw and hum, five times a day, into a half-filled bottle of water. For the first two weeks, I am diligent. I write "voice" on my calendar in the times before and after each meeting. I say *ohhhhhh* through a straw and hum up and down, like a siren.

At the end of a long day of teaching and marketing work, I hear scratchy gravel when I speak and worry that my efforts are for naught, though the therapist insists I sound better. But then I go on a trip, and I don't do the exercises five times a day. Three at most. Something, not nothing.

"I'm doing the best I can," I say to my husband.

Who am I trying to convince?

***

I search the calendar for a time to have surgery, after which I won't be able to speak for two weeks or teach for six. Maybe I won't have surgery. My voice sounds raspy, rough and stumbling, but I'm not in pain. A woman's voice deepens as she ages anyway.

"Try to vocally budget," the therapist says. "Limit the number of phone calls and Zooms. Avoid loud restaurants. If you have to strain your voice, do the exercises before and after."

When I cancel calls with friends, acquaintances, former clients, I feel relief. This may be the first time I've ever simplified my schedule.

You do too much, my grandmother used to say. I waved her away, believing I could do it all.

***

This isn't the first time my faltering voice alerted me to an uncomfortable truth.

At twenty-eight, I was engaged to be married. For weeks before the wedding, my fiancé, who was out of work, slept over every night, returning to his parents' house each morning, scruffy and untucked.

It took him seven years to finish college, but all he could talk about was the a cappella group he sang with on campus. Unable to hold a job for longer than nine months, he insisted he'd make it as a performing musician. I could be the partner who encouraged him to play piano and share his beautiful voice with the world. But when no one hired him for paying gigs, he curled into depression, and I panicked.

In a therapist's office, blinds drawn against the heat, I said, "I don't want to be the person who cancels the wedding. He'll go to therapy. I'll help him. I'll be the dutiful religious wife."

A religious wife puts her husband first. A Rebbetzin

told me to fake it in the bedroom, so my husband could find his pleasure. "You'll eventually have your chance," she said.

I emptied my closet of pants and short sleeves, wearing only long skirts, long sleeves, high-collared shirts. I bought fancy hats and cotton berets to cover my hair once we married. I even visited a wigmaker to consider buying an $1,800 human hair *sheitel*, backing out at the last minute because it was too heavy on my head.

We married before 350 people in black tie and floor-length dresses. At the reception, the band leader brought me to the side of the stage, and my husband got up with seven college friends to perform as if our wedding were a concert, as if all the people at the round tables were there to watch him sing and dance. It was August, and outside, the humidity was thick. Icy with air conditioning, the ballroom had no natural light. In my custom silk dress with little pearls on sheer sleeves, sequins in my curly hair, I forced a smile and tapped my hand against my dress, bopping to the music, embarrassed that everyone was witnessing my groom pull all focus from his bride.

But I should have expected it. For two weeks before the wedding, he stayed up every night, organizing the chuppah lighting, coordinating with the ceremony quartet, writing new music then balling it up and throwing it in the trash.

This was not a coming together of two souls; it was his grand debut. Marriage put him on the map, while it silenced and hid me away.

Later, in keeping with the rules of our religion, we danced on separate sides of the parquet. Men in black suits brought in chairs, lifting me up and carrying me to him, bouncing us in the air while everyone danced around us. Shaking with laughter, my husband handed me a white napkin to hold between us. I didn't get the joke.

In our hotel room that night, he explained, alight with laughter, that he had wiped his sweaty face with the napkin before giving it to me. I felt betrayed, tricked, the butt of an ugly joke. The last thing I wanted was him naked in my bed, but it was our wedding night, so I tried, until I had to push him away, saying, *it's okay if we just go to sleep,* when what I wanted to say was: *Let me close my eyes and shut you out.*

The first year of that marriage, my throat burned. Three times, the doctor diagnosed strep and prescribed antibiotics.

I sifted through the long skirts in my closet, ran my hands over the dozens of hats I wore to cover my hair. In the synagogue, I sat behind a wooden lattice with all the women. In that world, I'd forever be behind a barrier. From the front of the sanctuary, the rabbi called out page numbers. Men shuffled about mumbling prayers, slapping backs, sneaking shots of whiskey. Walking down the street on the Sabbath, I called "Good Shabbos!" to people I passed, but the men in black suits kept their eyes on their feet and scurried along without responding.

In intuitive medicine, getting sick in your throat means you feel you don't have a voice.

***

The four writing classes I teach every week include my signature course, Finding Your Voice. Through tears, my students say, "I need to claim my voice before it's too late. I have a lot to say. It's time to start saying it."

I know exactly what they mean.

***

Once, on a rooftop, in the moist heat of Bali, with views of bright green terraced rice paddies, a yoga instructor said, "You are enough, Lynne."

In the night, the wooden windows of my room flew open with urgent rains pounding from the sky. The wind was fierce and cool, a relief from the constant beating heat.

I stood at the windows, watching sheets of rain pour and pour. The dark storm was beautiful. Morning brought quiet and stillness, and though the ground was wet, the air was calm.

On that rooftop, I sat on a mat, holding a binder on life coaching. I was the instructor's guest, invited to write about her and photograph participants. Her words surprised me. I hadn't asked a question or encouraged scrutiny.

Standing in the open window, I wanted to stop telling other people's stories and get to know my own.

***

I've been working since I was fourteen. At my first job, Dunkin' Donuts on Orchard Lake Road, I wore the pink and orange uniform, packed donuts into boxes and poured coffee with two creams, two sugars, unless told otherwise.

I loved that job. I was in the world, meeting people, offering quippy conversation and a quick smile, and on my breaks, I drank hot chocolate with a shot of cream because I could eat anything and never gain weight.

After Dunkin', I worked at a dry cleaner and then I managed an aerobics studio, and then I went to college and collected more jobs, always doing what others demanded, even after I moved on from customer service. The minute I graduated, I drove to New York and lived in a small apartment with a friend from middle school and rode subways and buses to and from my job at a newspaper in the clanging city. I've been working for thirty-six years. I am a hard worker. Smart. A go-getter. All the words people use to describe me are about what I can do. Nothing about who I am. No wonder my voice falters. I learned to measure my value by how well I satisfied other people's needs. It's exhausting to always say what other people need to hear.

***

Researching the throat chakra, I learn its energy comes from effective communication, inspiration, expression, so if I don't follow my purpose or live authentically, a blockage will form.

I may never know what caused my injury. Perhaps the three-hour webinar I taught in November, or maybe just wear and tear and living lots of years. Because the polyp is small, the voice therapist says I may choose to live with it rather than remove it. It will never become cancerous. Besides, even with surgery, it could return.

***

In our final session, the voice therapist explains vocal fry—the huskiness at the end of a sentence, when the voice dips down and drags across the ground. *Try not to*, she says.

Working in Argentina, she noticed that Spanish-speakers finish sentences on a rise. Their voices go up, very little vocal fry.

But Americans fry our voices all the time. Our sentences descend into guttural endings. We are tough on the voice.

So I'll be quiet for a time and let my voice come through on the page, choosing my words to proclaim *I am absolutely enough, and it is time to be heard.*

This essay was first published in THE DILLYDOUN REVIEW on September 12, 2022. https://thedillydounre view.com/issue-20/lynne-golodner/

ACKNOWLEDGEMENTS

Once, years ago, a guy I was dating insisted that he didn't want me to write about him. "If you don't want me to write about you, you shouldn't fall in love with a writer," I replied.

Life is full of stories. Everywhere you go, everyone you meet. Through writing, I figure out what I believe, how I feel, process what happens in life. Writing is how I make sense of the world. I've always written about my experiences. This collection of creative nonfiction essays represents decades of my life, my coming-into-myself, and I am grateful to all those who have supported and continue to support my writing, who encourage me to write and to publish, and who believe in the power of story to connect us.

Thanks to Dan, the love of my life, who has always seen me as a writer. I am my best self because I share life with you. All my love to my four wonderful children—Asher, Eliana, Grace and Shaya. Though you never read my writing, you support my right to do it.

Thanks to my mother, Sonny Cohn, for championing my writing. You are a wonderful mother, a fantastic grandmother, and a great friend. I was very, very lucky to be raised by you.

Thank you always to my sister Jody Charlip, my aunt Suzanne Zwiren and my cousin Amanda Zwiren, for being great cheerleaders and some of the most special people in my life.

Thank you to Jessica Fein, Elizabeth Gowing, Danny Hankner, Kim Kozlowski and M.L. Liebler for blurbing this book. Thank you to my Michigan writers workshop, women I love deeply who have become an important part of my life— Susan Chaplin, Karen Hildebrandt, Pam Houghton, Kim Kozlowski, Carrie Nantais, Anne Osmer, Lisa Peers. You've helped many of these essays grow stronger and become publishable! Thank you to my Tuesday co-writing group—Janet Bailey, Elizabeth Gowing and Rachel Weikel—the kindest, most supportive and encouraging global group of friends I could ask for.

Thank you to Jenny Rarden, my fearless editor, who is always available and great at what she does. Thank you to Susan Jones and Patrick McEntaggart for another fantastic cover design. It is great fun to work with you. I am grateful to the Women's Fiction Writers Association and all the friends I've made there who are the best support system an author could ask for.

ABOUT THE AUTHOR

Lynne Golodner is the author of eleven books and thousands of articles as well as a marketing entrepreneur, writing coach and retreat leader. (Lynne's work has been published with three different surnames: Lynne Cohn, Lynne Schreiber and Lynne Golodner.) After working as a journalist in New York and Washington, D.C., Lynne returned to her native Detroit to pursue a freelance writing career and teach writing. In 2007, she created Your People LLC, a marketing and public relations company with a focus on storytelling that helps companies, organizations and entrepreneurs build their brands and market their work.

Lynne's writing has appeared in *Saveur*, the *Chicago Tribune*, *Better Homes and Gardens*, *Midwest Living*, the *Detroit Free Press*, *Porridge Magazine*, the *Jewish Literary Journal*, *The Good Life Review*, *Hadassah Magazine*, *The Forward*, *Valiant Scribe*, *Story Unlikely*, *The Dillydoun Review*, *QuibbleLit* and *YourTango*, among many more publications.

Among the awards she has won for her writing, Lynne's first novel, WOMAN OF VALOR, won an honorable mention in the Spiritual Fiction category of the Eric Hoffer Awards, and one of her essays was a 2022 finalist in the Annie Dillard Award for Creative Nonfiction through *The Bellingham Review*. Lynne's second novel, CAVE OF SECRETS, earned the #1 spot on Amazon in Jewish fiction, Gay Fiction and British and Irish Literature.

Lynne teaches writing around the world. A former Fulbright Specialist, she is a graduate of the University of Michigan (BA, Communications/English) and Goddard College (MFA, Poetry). The mother of four young adults, Lynne lives in Huntington Woods, Michigan with her archivist husband Dan.

Learn more at https://lynnegolodner.com.